Cover Art

Ek Onkar

One Creator that manifests It Self in Its Creation reflecting the spiritual unity, interconnectedness and interdependence of life on this planet. The Circle surrounded by crossed swords signifies the eternal spiritual Force that protects the unprotected and promotes justice and fair play.

Planet Earth

Our home sweet home. Humanity's one and only home.

The Beauty that Surrounds Us
The mystical wonder of Muir Woods in California on a rainy day.

A visual expresion by a student of their experience of my class on Spiritual Paths.

Changing the Course of Destruction
Listening to Understand Each Other In-Depth Promotes Peace

by R.K. Janmeja (Meji) Singh, Ph.D.

Editors:
Joginder Singh Ahluwalia, Ingenieur Doctéur, Gyani
John Hazen, M.A., MFT

Director of Publications
Chris Celio, Psy.D.

ISBN: 1978228023
ISBN-13: 978-1978228023

Available at Amazon.com in Paperback and Kindle formats.

Table of Contents

Preface

Meji and I have been friends for over 10 years because of our common interest in serving our fellow human beings. Much of that time I spent in assisting Portia Bell Hume Behavioral Health and Training Center to obtain grants to sustain and expand their services. Meji is the Founding President, 1993. Hume Center is a behavioral health center serving Alameda and Contra Costa Counties located in the San Francisco East Bay Area. I have also served with him as an Officer of the Ik Onkar Peace Foundation. Meji is the founding President of this Cooperation Circle in a worldwide network of United Religions Initiative (URI), having 850 such circles in over 101 different countries.

The majority of content in this book consists of papers written over a period of over 20 years by Meji in response to events ranging from the Partition of India in 1947 to Hitler's Germany to the September 11, 2001 attack on The World Trade Center in New York and their relevance to our current geopolitical situation. This preface is my attempt to provide the reader with a brief description of the underlying concepts and how they link from Meji's premise to his proposed methods to solve geopolitical problems. The papers themselves in most cases provide the reader with further elaboration and context regarding the conceptual framework and underlying processes.

On the basis of his experience as a clinical psychologist and an organizational development consultant he has found that the problems presented are never the problem. To solve a presented problem one has to identify the underlying processes of which the person(s) presenting the problem are usually unaware. The same is true of geopolitical problems. The parties solving the international political conflicts are using the same methods to solve the problems that created the problems in the first place.

The world is on a course of destruction because we do not pay attention to the underlying processes that create the problem. One simple example is the geopolitical striving motivated by our misconceived sectarian self-interest and fear of the "other." Constant promotion of consumption to increase wealth for a relatively small percentage of the world's population is at the expense of human health and wellbeing.

Understanding Destructive Geopolitical Conflicts: In his academic and professional service experience as a clinical Psychologist, inspired by the teaching and mentoring of Gerald Caplan M.D., Professor of Psychiatry, Harvard School of Public Health, Meji subsequently expanded understanding and uses of his theory and practice of Consultation. Caplan developed the theory and practice that a community mental health consultant could alleviate the unconscious theme interference in a problematic interaction in one or two sessions. Meji has been practicing Community Behavioral Health Consultation for more than half a century. He found that this practice is equally effective in organizational conflicts and international conflicts. He described his conceptual model of Organizational Dynamics in a paper titled Beyond Camelot. This conceptual framework helps us understand that in organizations, including political movements, internal and external pressures (e.g. poverty, the organization of work, faulty internalized cultural values, nutritional practices and uneven availability of health care) and the structures and processes that deal with such pressures have usually a more important role in behavioral outcomes than personal psychodynamics. Meji applies this framework to help us understand the dynamics that shaped outcomes in Nazi Germany, U.S. politics in the 20th and 21st century and in the 20th century struggle for freedom by the peoples of India and Pakistan.

Integrative View. Growing up in India as a Sikh (itself a religion of acceptance of diversity) and having spent more than half a century in the States, Meji, throughout his lifetime has made serious inquiry into the most well known original spiritual guides (the Sikh Gurus, Sufis, Bhagats, Moses, Christ and Muhammad). He observes that fundamental values and messages are in common among all these sages. Integrating theories of psychology and the teaching of original spiritual guides, Meji understands "human nature" as a dynamic of conscious and unconscious elements that manifest in a balance or imbalance with misconceived self-interest and fear of the "other." To explore this Meji, describes Haumain and Cain consciousness.

In the course of building support for particular political ends, leaders (and their adherents) have historically adopted certain methods and processes to exploit the population's fears, feelings of disenfranchisement and attachment to sectarian interests to divide them. The methods incorporate religion, patriotism, racism and scapegoating. Meji sees that these phenomena are better understood from a system dynamics perspective than through the lens of personal psychodynamics alone.

The Opportunity

This point in history may be the perfect opportunity for commitment to and application of methodology to resolve conflicts in a non-violent way. With humankind's ever enlarging footprint on mother Earth causing climate change, with our mutual capacity through technology to use weapons of mass destruction, we may be at a threshold of motivation to take the opportunity to save ourselves. Survival of us as a species requires now that political and economic leadership direct work, health and educational institutions to promote the overall wellbeing of humanity instead of misconceived shortsighted sectarian or regional interests.

Based upon the knowledge we now have of ourselves as individuals and social entities (organizations, socio-political-economic structures, etc.) we have individuals and groups trained and appropriate to act as facilitators for healthy change. Collaterally, Meji assesses that most political discourse is centered on solving political problems as presented. He makes a crucial observation that the problem as presented is never the problem and those methods that caused or sustained the problem continue to be used to solve it. Yet, currently we have the knowledge and consultants have the expertise to facilitate successful and sustainable solutions. Meji describes this "technology" in the Consultation model as it applies to individuals and to organizations, including political-economic entities.

I encourage the reader to enjoy each of Meji's papers for their resonance and contribution to your own point of view. None of his papers are intended as scientific or political position papers. His integration of learning from spiritual guides (not religions) and intra-psychic and system dynamics has provided me with a rich set of lenses to understand modern socio-economic and political evolution. I find it particularly fascinating to read Meji's perceptions as a child and young adult during the years around birth of Pakistan as a partition of India. Meji ranks as a quickly disappearing few with such intimate experience of this jolting and traumatic historic event and fewer yet who have analyzed this chapter of history for its lessons to learn for the rest of us.

John Hazen, M.A., MFT

Thanks

I am thankful to the tens and thousands of persons whose loving presence has been a constant source of life and inspiration to me. To name a few is a distortion of reality. I am most thankful to the Director, the Creator of this life, who gave me a very wonderful and exciting role, who blessed me with the parents, sisters, brothers, friends and teachers who through their nurturing guidance introduced me to sports, studies, literature, arts and culture and most of all to Baba Guru Nanak-Guru Gobind Singh. These Gurus showed me the path of spiritual unity of the universe, inspired me to enjoy and preserve nature and lead a life of service. They have helped me to realize that I am a part of the Divine order and not a cause of it. I just play my role in this cosmic play and go back to my Creator.

The Director chose to give me Punjab as a land of my birth where I could enjoy a diverse society, the Sufi saints, the poetry of Punjabi and Urdu poets and the tragedy of betrayal by the political leadership and poisoning of people's minds with divisiveness. Over a million persons were murdered and eighteen million people were forced to leave their ancestral homes, neighbors and friends during the Partition of India. I am thankful that my journey took me to the United States and even the experience of the Nine Eleven tragedy. Here I have been introduced to another exciting culture, arts, literature, and history. I was given the opportunity to study human behavior, discover unconscious dynamics and helped to understand psychological processes affecting human behavior and how this applies to the global socio-political and economic system. The Director has provided me with the opportunities and means to experience fully whatever I was given to do. **No words can express the sense of my gratitude!**

For the publication of this book I am thankful to Dr. Joginder Singh Ahluwalia, who not only edited the book but has also been my mentor. I learned from him immensely. He spent an enormous amount of time making corrections. I thank Mr. John Hazen for doing the final editing of the book. But for Dr. Chris Celio's encouragement and support, I would have never collected my writings to publish them. I want to thank Dr. Bruce McAuley and his team at Sequoia Hospital in Redwood City who has been my cardiologist since my heart attack 36 years ago and to my Internist Dr. Naras Bhat in Concord, CA.

Dedicated to the Peoples of this World

and

Presented to the Ruling Elite, the political and religious leaders, journalists, academicians and the CEOs of multinational corporations for their consideration if they see the necessity of change and have the willingness to pursue it.

Introduction

Kya Hooa Agar Murkz-e-Hasti Insaan Na Hua

Abroo Khaak Hai Katra Ki Jo Toofan Na Hua

Sharam Bhi Ati Hai Aur Afsos Bhi Hota Hai

Admi Youn To Sabhi Kuch Hua Magar Insaan Na Hua

Hain Mere Dil Mein Voh Aahen Jo Na Bani Bilee

Meri Aankhon Mein Voh Katra Hai Jo Toofan Na Hua

What does it matter if the focus of existence is not being human?

A drop is nothing if it did not become a storm

It is a matter of shame and a feeling of sorrow

Man became everything but never could become a human being

I have sighs within me that never became lightening

I have a drop in my eyes that never became a storm

Kaifi

About forty years ago when I lived in Berkeley, California I got a dining room set and a coffee table made of Sheesham wood with an inlay work of mixed metal bronze. Every day I got such a joy from having this set. It was made in a remote village: Chaneot in Pakistan. I have never met the craftsman, so I couldn't share with him the joy it has brought in my life. If I lived in the same village I would have run into him every day. During my morning walk or evening stroll or going to Bazar. I might have said Assalamu-alaikum, talked to him, told his children what a wonderful craftsman their Abba Jaan was and how grateful I am to him for what he created for me. My friends here like my dining set and ask me how much did it cost? Carl Marx had predicted that when goods are mass-produced, human labor will become a commodity and it will have a profound impact on social relationships. The maker of this furniture is a commodity measured in the cost of his labor and the human interaction is lost.

In Dublin I live in a very nice, quiet neighborhood. I know nobody. I have a lot of friends but I have to drive from 20 minutes to more than an hour or fly thousands of miles to visit them. I have enough financial resources to buy anything I want. These are all financial transactions. The human being is a commodity involved in manufacturing, marketing and selling the moneylender's goods to their consumers. The moneylenders hire people of all walks of life including the politicians, clergy, journalists, academicians, artists, professionals and administrators to do their bidding. Now they have hired scientists and technologists to replace this human commodity with robots. They do not talk back or go on strike. The moneylenders can have better return for their money without any hassles. This is a great civilization replacing human civilization!

At age 86 my life is full of warm memories of kind and loving people I have met and the beauty and mystery I experienced in nature and its ever-changing manifestations. The cultural events and the sports that I participated in have enriched my life. My professional and material successes and failures have been quite an adventure. Now, I am wondering where I started and the kind of civilization I lived in and where human civilization is headed? It makes me shudder when I think of the future. **We are at the crossroads. We can make this planet a heavenly abode, or keep sleep walking into our own destruction if we do not wake up and change the current course of our geopolitical striving motivated by our misconceived self-interest and creating fear of the "other."**

My life has been deeply impacted by the 1947 Partition of India. I could not understand how such a horrific tragedy could take place. I see this tragedy is still being repeated every day all over the world. I was given the professional interest in studying human behavior as a part of my interest in understanding human suffering. The four essays in this book reflect my efforts to understand this tragedy within the socio-political and economic environment we live in. They were written during different times in my life and in a different context but I find a similar theme in all of them.

All the famous rulers, conquerors and political leaders have made contributions to the modern civilization. We also need to learn from the misguided motivation and mistakes they made and not just glorify them and get attached to them because they belong to our community or country. Instead of hero worship, **detached learning** may help us change the past dysfunctional and destructive paradigm of our civilization. If you love your country and support it right or wrong; if you adore the founders of your country and you are unconditionally grateful to them; if you are too proud of your religion and look down upon other religions; if you think that your values and thoughts are the best; if you are deeply attached to all of the above, you may have a very hard time reading this book as its major focus is to study our past history with **compassionate detachment,** to learn from it and not to worship it.

We have come a long way. This is a very exciting time. There is hope that the persons who promote humanistic values may become a majority and the "poor shall inherit the earth." It does not mean the poor in material sense but those who are detached from material egocentric (Haumain) pursuits at the cost of others and live in a loving consciousness and gratitude to our Creator for giving us this wonderful planet to experience life, to serve others and enjoy and preserve this beautiful creation. We need to be guided by our spiritual guides (I do not mean religion). **That means the focus on personal transformation to create human beings that can create a loving society.** Such a society will have leaders that are caring and compassionate, who serve their communities and have the intent and the skills to solve conflicts in a non-violent and peace promoting way.

These four essays are a summary of my observations and experience of my life on this planet and are presented as a humble offering to you for your review. I have repeatedly mentioned in this book that we have the knowledge and skills to resolve intra-psychic, interpersonal, intra-group, inter-group, national and inter-national conflicts in a peaceful and productive ways. But I had not discussed any of those. After receiving feedback on my first draft, I have added a chapter: The Presented Problem is never the Problem. In the next four volumes that will follow this book, I will try to summarize what I have learned in providing community behavioral health services to the communities I have served.

Being a community psychologist and an American Sikh, who was born in Punjab, has contributed a lot to the way I look at history. Therefore, it is essential for me to introduce you briefly to my experience in both of these aspects so that you may have the context of my point of view in understanding India's freedom struggle.

I was born in Montgomery (now called Sahiwal in Pakistan) Punjab, in 1931 in a Sikh family where my father was the Farm Manager of the Punjab Government Agriculture Farm. I spent my childhood in Resaale

Wala Farm. He was transferred to Lyallpur (now called Faisalabad) because of his promotion to be the Extra Assistant Director of Agriculture. Around 1938 he was transferred to Amritsar. He retired in 1946 and built a small house in Rupar rather than going to our nearby ancestral village, Kheri Salabat Pur. I finished my high school education there. I had to interrupt my college studies because we had very little income from our land and my father's retirement was held back because all the documents were in Lahore, Pakistan due to the partition of India.

My oldest brother, the late Professor Dr. T.S. Saini, took me to Kulu where he was working as a forest ranger before coming to the States. There I privately studied for the Gyani Examination. It is a diploma in Punjabi literature. I passed the Gyani examination from Punjab University in 1948 before joining Mahendra College, Patiala, for my undergraduate studies. I went to join the Punjab University Camp College in New Delhi to accomplish a Masters in Psychology. Afterward I taught at Malwa Teachers Training College in Ludhiana for a year. Having spent my twenty-five years in Punjab I came to the United States to do my Doctoral Studies in Clinical Psychology at Boston University in 1958 and I have been living and practicing in the States ever since.

I should let you know that I am not too fond of current psychiatric or mental health practice. Less than 11% of psychiatrists provide psychotherapy. Mostly they focus on symptoms and treat them with extensive use of psychotropic drugs. The Psychologists have taken to short cuts to psychotherapy and have developed numerous psycho-educational interventions. Managed Care may have some benefits but rules for "Quality Control" are misguided and at times approach ethical and legal limits, with directives for clinical practice without ever seeing the patient or lacking qualification to make treatment recommendations.

My clinical practice has included mostly providing psychotherapy to individuals, groups and families. I also have provided behavioral health consultation to organizations to create a more psychologically healthy and productive work environment. I have specialized in providing comprehensive community behavioral health services with continuity of care from primary prevention programs in the community to secondary prevention by providing clinical services to persons whose behavior has become dysfunctional and quality of life for them has become quite unsatisfactory. We have developed tertiary prevention programs for after care or rehabilitation services for persons with serious mental disorders to reintegrate into the community. I specialize in preventing, resolving or managing conflicts at intra-psychic, interpersonal, organizational, inter-agency and inter-community levels.

When an individual came to me for psychotherapy, she/he created their psychological reality in relationship to me. How I responded to the reality they created in relationship to me determined how much their behavior would change for their own benefit. **To make an appropriate response I needed to understand the symbolic significance of their behavior and how it represents their intra-psychic reality that was created by the pain and suffering they have experienced in their socio-economic, political and cultural context and the kind of coping mechanisms they have developed to deal with that suffering.** Through this journey through their inner life, **they learned new and more satisfying ways to deal with their suffering.** Just having a conversation about their manifest behavior or symptoms was not very useful. **It is through this work I understand the importance of the socio-economic, political, academic and spiritual environment we live in. We as a community are responsible for the dysfunctional behavior of the individuals that I have seen in psychotherapy.**

My spiritual orientation is briefly described under the title Freedom from One's Self in the chapter on Did India and Pakistan Win Freedom? **Using the psycho-spiritual paradigm to understand the history of freedom struggle of India one has to understand the symbolic significance of the manifest content of the struggle for freedom in terms of the persons and events involved.** Since I am not asked to consult with anyone engaged in bringing about change, the purpose is not to bring about change but to contribute a different kind of awareness that may create a need for change and help the political change agents to develop systems and institutions in their efforts to bring peace and happiness on this planet. If they deem it appropriate to hire my colleagues, trained in conflict resolution at the intra-psychic, interpersonal, community, organizational or international political conflicts level they may contribute to having a more functional and satisfying paradigm of human civilization. It is obvious that the current paradigm of civilization, in spite of certain improvements, is still quite a failure and has brought immense suffering to humanity and destruction on this planet.

In my view all expressions of an individual are a manifestation of all the influences on a person. **The point is, are the basic facts correct?** It is important for the person to know that my point of view is informed by my interest in understanding the spiritual (not religious) inheritance of human civilization, my interest in Urdu, Punjabi and English literature, pursuit of Indian and Western Philosophy in addition to my practice as a community psychologist. I have been trying to heal human suffering in individuals, families and human organizations. Such suffering is the result of the psycho-spiritual, socio-economic and political environment we live in. If someone just gets hooked into a single aspect of my being, it will be their unfortunate attachment to a limited view of the total reality of my being. Such tendencies to getting hooked into one aspect of a person or a situation impedes a comprehensive understanding of a person or the organization or point of view they represent. To develop a deeper understanding of a person or a community one needs time, investment, effort and skills to listen and understand.

Chapter – I

CHANGING THE COURSE
OF DESTRUCTION

This paper was presented at the Fourth Annual Convention of the Congress of Political Economists at Paris, January 8-13, 1993.

This paper is a personal statement. I also want you to read it keeping in mind the backdrop of your personal experience and your observations about the country you represent. You may evaluate the issues raised in this paper to see if they fit into the way you have experienced the country with which you are most familiar. Please do not read this paper with the usual "scientific objective distance." It is the responsibility of each one of us to participate in determining the course of human destiny no matter what our field of endeavor is. The wellbeing of humanity and the planet is our common concern. You need to formulate for yourself where you stand on the issues discussed in this paper without waiting for a definitive study on any of the points made. Regardless of whatever theories or scientific evidence that is to come, the human race continues to move in one direction or the other. Each of us has to make the best possible individual judgment in order to chalk the course of human destiny on the basis of the best possible data available to us through our own life experience.

I am privileged to present my ideas to this august body because you deal with the production and distribution of goods and services that are necessary for life and have the most potent effect on human destiny. In Indian philosophical literature, Maya stands for wealth and is also used for illusion in the sense that the material world has its own reality that is as illusionary as it is impermanent. The material world is transitory in contrast to spiritual reality that is eternal.

These two realities are integral in relationship. Political economists hold the key for bringing social responsibility and spiritual perspective to satisfy economic needs.

I lived in Punjab, India, for 25 years and received my Master's degree in Psychology from Punjab University Camp College, New Delhi, before I came to the United States in 1958. I was trained as a clinical psychologist from 1958-64. At that time psychoanalysis was at its peak. Most of my professors and supervisors who influenced my clinical practice were psychoanalysts.

I developed a sound foundation to understand the nature of unconscious motivation and its impact on our intra-psychic processes and interpersonal relationships. My training provided me with an effective framework with which to alleviate the disruptive influence of unconscious processes on behavior through individual and group psychotherapy practice. In 1963, I attended two semester seminars on Community Mental Health Consultation with Gerald Caplan, M.D., Professor of Psychiatry at Harvard School of Public Health. He put forth the theory and practice of Mental Health Consultation that one could alleviate the unconscious interference in a problematic interaction in one or two sessions in his book Principles of Preventive Psychiatry (Caplan, 1964). I became the Assistant Director of the Center for training in Community Psychiatry, Berkeley started by Portia Bell Hume, M.D., where I have used Caplan's theory and techniques of consultation in resolving conflicts at individual, family and organizational levels (Singh 1971, 1975 and 1989). I have devoted my professional life in developing technologies and a conceptual framework for consultation practice.

On the basis of my 30 years of clinical and consultation experience, **I have come to the conclusion that it is much more productive to use a systems approach rather than an individual study approach in order to understand human history in order to change the course of destruction we have been following.** My model of system dynamics is presented in a paper entitled, "Beyond Camelot: Making Work a Growth-Stimulating Situation" (Singh 1975). In spite of my training in psychoanalytic psychotherapy, I came to a very different conclusion on the basis of my practice as an Organizational Development Consultant regarding the interpersonal tensions and conflicts, poor morale and low productivity that is found in organizations:

> **The interpersonal tensions in an organization have very little to do with the individuals and their intra-psychic processes. Individuals are relevant but are not the cause of the appearance of such tensions. These tensions are a result of the unresolved stresses impinging on the organization.** (Singh, 1975)

The resolution of the pressures on an organization depends on the structures and processes available to the organization to resolve such pressures. **The system dynamic model summarized above may also be more productive in understanding national and international tensions and in providing consultative help to prevent destructive outcomes.** It is not unusual that a national leader will take a country to war as one means of resolving the internal problems that he or she might find very difficult to resolve in any other way.

Frustration leads to aggression. In the case of war, the frustrations caused by the inability to resolve the pressures on the organization are released through fighting an external enemy. Each organization (or nation) resolves the pressures impinging on it in its own unique way. I have chosen the most blatant example from recent history, Hitler's Germany, to contrast the two approaches to understand the national phenomenon. One analyzes the personality of the leader and the other uses the system dynamics approach.

I want to make the reader aware that the system dynamics analysis presented in the following pages does not represent the actual analysis, as it would reveal itself through the consultation process. Organizational consultation is an interactional process (Singh, 1989) between the consultant and the consultee that simultaneously identifies and resolves a particular problem. Quite often the consultee is not even aware of how the problem got resolved. 99% of the time, the way the problem is formulated and presented to the consultant is not the real problem. However, the following example is to demonstrate that in addition to personality there were numerous system variables that contributed to the development of Hitler, his rise to power and his destructive influence prior to and during World War II.

The Personality Analysis Approach

One of the most respected psychoanalysts, Erik Erikson, summarized epithets used to describe Hitler before he presented his explanation:

> **I shall now review the psychiatric literature which has described Hitler as a 'psychopathic paranoid,' an 'amoral sadistic infant,' an 'over compensatory sissy' or a 'neurotic laboring under the compulsion to murder.' At times, he undoubtedly was all that. But, unfortunately, he**

was something over and above it all.

Erikson, 1963

Most of the above reaction is more of counter-transference phenomenon rather than developing a psychological understanding that may lead to preventive approach.

In the following paragraph, Erikson explains away the destruction caused by Hitler attributing it

> **...to a psychoanalytic interpretation of the first chapter of MEIN KAMPF as an involuntary confession of Hitler's Oedipus complex. This interpretation would suggest that, in Hitler's case, the love for his young mother and the hate for his old father assumed morbid proportions, and it was this conflict which drove him to love and to hate and compelled him to save or destroy people and peoples who really stand for his mother and his father.**

In the latter part of his chapter on "The Legend of Hitler's Childhood," he refers to some forces of history to further his theory that it was the perfect fit between the adolescent identity crisis of Hitler and the German nation:

> **Naturally, this account is made typical to the point of caricature. Yet I believe that both the overt type and the covert pattern existed and that, in fact, this regular split between preconscious individualistic rebellion and disillusioned, obedient citizenship was a strong factor in the political immaturity of the German. This adolescent rebellion was an aboration of individualism and revolutionary spirit.**

Erikson also makes the point that the German nation was not as evolved as the other European nations. In the following quote, he compares Germans to Americans:

> **On such a foundation Hitler offered a simple racial dichotomy of cosmic dimensions; the German (soldier) versus the Jew. The Jew is described as small, black, and hairy all over; his back is bent, his feet are flat; his eyes squint, and his lips smack; he has an evil smell, is**

**promiscuous, and loves to deflower and impregnate, and infect blond
girls. The Aryan is tall, erect, light, without hair on chest and limbs...**

Erikson concludes:

> **This antithesis is clearly one of ape man and superman. But while
> in this country such imagery may have made comics, in Germany it
> became official food for adult minds.**

What Erikson fails to recognize in his statement is that every racist culture has a very similar description of the people it discriminates against.
In the U.S. very similar stereotypes are prevalent in racist circles about
African Americans, and such imagery is not considered comical. Hitler
did not invent racist imagery or racism. I will discuss such imagery and
racism at length later in this paper. Michael Parenti (1992) refers to the
4th Century Greeks:

> **The Greeks desecrated foreigners, better known as barbarians. They
> were accorded the contemptuous term, Andropada, which means a
> man-footed creature or man-footed animal.**

Hitler's view of Jews was not an exception. Racists have always justified their atrocities by dehumanizing and denigrating their victims all
through history and across all continents. There is some truth to the
fact that leaders exploit the psychological vulnerability of their people.
Nevertheless, Eriksonian analysis is too limited and misleading. The
pressures prevalent on the German nation at the time of Hitler and
the structures and processes used to deal with those pressures are still
around. Such structures and processes were in use before Hitler was
born and they continue being used since his death by the power elite in
almost all countries. Not because they are bad people but mainly because they did not and do not know any better. In most cases the leaders
genuinely believe in what they say and do as the best choice for their
people.

Hitler is Alive, Well, and Prospering in Every Country

If we analyze Hitler and Germany in terms of the pressures impinging
upon a country and its ability to deal with those pressures productively,

we may decrease our chances of repeating the same event over and over again. Hitler's autobiography, MEIN KAMPF, provides very valuable data because it provides "...a self- revelation of such overwhelming frankness..." (Konrad Heiden in his introduction to MEIN KAMPF, 1925).

Hitler described in his autobiography his life, political philosophy and political strategy, and also the processes that transformed his views and actions as well.

Erikson's analysis may have validity and the reader is referred to his CHILDHOOD AND SOCIETY (Erikson, 1963). Hitler became a very stubborn individual, a characteristic he may have acquired from his father who was stubborn and punitive. Hitler's mother was nurturing and loving. Have you ever come across a punitive father and a nurturing and loving mother? No matter which country or culture we come from, we need to look at how we parent our children: with love and intimacy or with fear and punishment.

Karl Menninger wrote his book, CRIME OF PUNISHMENT (Menninger, 1966), and he was not writing about Hitler or the German people. The psychological literature is replete with studies that show how punitive child rearing is related to all kinds of neurotic, addictive or delinquent behavior. Today, it is common knowledge that abusive parents were usually abused when they were children. It is misleading to limit this analysis to Hitler or Germany. Child abuse is a universal phenomenon. Psychoanalysts make a common mistake when they generalize their insights. They select in and select out data to confirm their "insights." (I intentionally choose the term insight here, rather than hypothesis.) If we only look at the resolution of the Oedipus complex and the relationship to mother and father, our insights may be correct but limited, and we may not arrive at adequate preventive solutions.

Poverty

Hitler points to the living conditions of the poor working class and to his own experience of poverty in MEIN KAMPF:

> **While the goddess of suffering took me in her arms, often threatening to crush me, my will to resistance grew, and in the end this will was**

victorious.

Five years in which I was forced to earn a living, first as a day laborer, then as a small painter; a truly meager living which never sufficed to appease even my daily hunger. Hunger was then my faithful bodyguard; he never left me for a moment and partook of all I had, share and share alike. Every book I acquired aroused his interest; a visit to the opera prompted his attentions for days at a time; my life was a continuous struggle with this pitiless friend.

By forcing me to return to this world of poverty and insecurity, from which my father had risen in the course of his life, it removed the blinders of a narrow petty bourgeois upbringing from my eyes. Only now did I learn to know humanity, learning to distinguish between empty appearances or brutal external and inner being.

In the light of his experience, Hitler began to see the plight of the poor in the following way:

> The consequence is that once the man obtains work he irresponsibly forgets all of order and discipline, and begins to live luxuriously for the pleasure of the moment. This upsets even the small weekly budget, as even here any intelligent apportionment is lacking; in the beginning it suffices for five days instead of seven, later only for three, finally scarcely for one day, and in the end it is drunk up in the very first night.

> Often he has a wife and children at home. Sometimes they, too, are infected by this life, especially when the man is good to them on the whole and actually loves them in his own way. Then the weekly wage are used up by the whole family in two or three days; they eat and drink as long as the money holds out and the last days they go hungry. Then the wife drags herself out into the neighborhood, borrows a little, runs up little debts at the food store, and in this way strives to get through the hard last days of the week. At noon they all sit together before their meager and sometimes empty bowls, waiting for the next pay day, speaking of it, making plans, in their hunger, dreaming of the happiness to come.

I am sure that you have witnessed such poverty where you come from. In the U.S., the richest country in the world, with regard to the millions of homeless people, 20% of the requests for food at homeless shelters go unfulfilled, and 23% of the requests for such shelter cannot be met. Hitler had not seen this kind of poverty in his life, yet he warned us:

> **What was--and still is--bound to happen someday, when the stream of unleashed slaves pours forth from these miserable dens to avenge themselves on their thoughtless fellow men!**

In the United States, this happened in the 1960's on a mass scale. It happened in May 1992 in the Los Angeles riots. It happens every day in street violence and police brutality.

Poverty is built into modern economic structure. President Reagan had a trickle-down theory and appealed to American volunteerism. Hitler had the following to say about volunteer social work:

> **Consequently, and much to their own amazement, the result of their social 'efforts' is always nil; frequently, in fact, an indignant rebuff; though this, of course, is passed off as a proof of the people's ingratitude.**

> **Such minds are most reluctant to realize that social endeavor has nothing in common with this sort of thing; that above all it can raise no claim to gratitude, since its function is not to distribute favors but to restore rights.**

> **The more I witnessed it, the greater grew my revulsion for the big city which first sucked men in and then so cruelly crushed them.**

Hitler bemoaned the loss of the ownership of private property and the weakening of the peasant class:

> **A grave economic symptom of decay was the slow disappearance of the right to private property, and the gradual transference of the entire economy to the ownership of stock companies.**

> **The first consequence of gravest importance was the weakening of the peasant class, proportionately as the peasant class diminished, the mass of big city proletariat increased more and more, until finally the balance was completely upset.**

During the last 12 years in the United States, thousands of family farms have been foreclosed, unemployment has been at its highest, and small family businesses are becoming an extinct institution. I am not an economist. I just have a question: Why is it that Yale, Harvard, Oxford, etc. train economists to create or contribute to such awful economic conditions? Why is it that it took almost a century before a small Congress of Political Economists was organized?

I wish you all gathered here the best of luck! As a psychologist, my point is simply to bring to your attention a more comprehensive system dynamics model for analysis of national and international events.

According to the method of analysis I outlined in "Beyond Camelot," we also need to look at the pressures impinging on a family. To begin with, there are internal pressures that come from internalized cultural values that may be faulty. Then, there are external pressures that impact the behavior of the individuals within the family. Poverty and work organization create a major stress on the family system, which is often ignored even by family therapy theorists. There is evidence that working "graveyard" or night shifts leads to more health problems, divorce and child abuse. Economic difficulties, health problems, non-availability of health care, poor diet, among others factors, all can affect the family interaction. I do not mean to suggest that poverty itself determines the outcome of family relationships. However, poverty accentuates and precipitates the negative outcomes. External pressures are not limited to poverty. Family interaction could be affected, for example, by the great success of one family member. He/she may be so caught up in his/her professional or monetary success that it jeopardizes the intimate and loving care of the children and jeopardizes family stability in general.

It is incumbent upon political economists to study the organization of work not just in terms of production of goods and services but also in terms of human cost. Let money not be the measure of all things but let human wellbeing be the focus of all analytical endeavor!

These days, the single working parent is under far more stress than an old fashioned extended or nuclear family. What do we need to do to reduce the pressures on the family so that it provides a loving and nurturing environment? Each family has its unique pressures and its resources to deal with those pressures. Rich families are not necessarily more nurturing. For example, child abuse is found in families across all socio-economic and educational levels. We need to study pressure systems on families and develop programs to reduce these pressures. If we have the attitude of the former U.S. Vice President, Mr. Dan Quale, that the persons who rioted in Los Angeles are responsible for the Los Angeles riots, then we are doomed to destruction.

If, like Erik Erikson, we fail to take note of the living conditions of Hitler, or of any of the rest of us, then we are off the track to bring about productive change.

There is a flaw in focusing on individual psychopathology that is a result of the psychosocial history of the individual. As a political leader the person is a part of the national history in the context of global socio-economic and political history as it is manifested in the present socio-economic-political environment. To change the course of destruction one has to take such a comprehensive approach to understand the complexity of the problem. Only then we can find an adequate solution.

Religion as the Tool of the Power Elite

> **Worst of all, however, is the devastation wrought by the misuse of religious conviction for political ends. In truth, we cannot sharply enough attack those wretched crooks who would like to make religion an implement to perform political or rather business services for them (Hitler, 1925).**

Have we stopped using religion for political purposes or for personal gain? In fact, historically there is hardly any relationship between spirituality and religion. Spirituality is a very personal effort toward the spiritual development of the individual. Traditionally, religion has hindered more than helped the spiritual development of its followers. For example, there is hardly any relationship between "Christ consciousness" and Christianity. Leaving aside history, just in October of last year during the 500th anniversary of Columbus's discovery of America, Pope Paul exalted Columbus for bringing Christianity to the Americas. Can you visualize Christ accompanying Columbus to the eventual wholesale massacre of indigenous Americans or, earlier, Christ accompanying the Crusaders to plunder other nations?

During the Gulf War, both Presidents Saddam Hussein and George Bush were shown on TV praying or going to church.

In the United States during the 1992 Republican convention, the prime time speakers criticized the Democrats for not mentioning God, while Republicans, in the name of God, presented the most exclusionary platform in modern memory. In India, you have seen the politicians exploiting the populace for their political gains making an issue of a non-issue with regard to the Babri Masjid and Ram Temple, Rajeev Gandhi started his political campaign from Ayodhya, the mythical place of Lord Ram's birth, to get votes from the Hindu fundamentalists. The Bhartya Janta party made this their major issue, which does nothing to solve the real problems of living or the spiritual development of the people. Awasthi et al has discussed this in detail in a cover article of INDIA TODAY. (Awasthi, 1992). To maintain her political power, Mrs. Indira Gandhi used Sikhs as a scapegoat. It is a very well-known fact that she planted Sant Jarnail Singh Bhindrawala[1] to destroy the political hold of the Akali party over the Sikh Gurdwaras[2], which provided economic and political resources for Akali political leadership. She supported his violence and helped him fortify the Golden Temple complex. Gupta et al, in INDIA TODAY (August 15, 1991), described a panel discussion in which this well-known fact was further confirmed by the insiders in Mrs. Gandhi's government. In this panel discussion organized by India Today, Mr. Vasant Sathe, the Information and Broadcasting Minister in Mrs. Gandhi's cabinet, stated:

As Information and Broadcasting Minister, I told Indira ji, 'Let Bhindrawala's supporters speak on television. Speak to your colleagues.' They said: 'Sathe ji, you keep out of it. He is our own man. We brought him only to break the Akalis. The day we want we will fix him.'

Before Sant Bhindrawala, almost all the opposition parties supported

---

1	He was from a small village and had a great following for his spiritual work. Mrs. Gandhi brought him into politics for her political purposes.
2	Sikh place of learning.

the Akali party's political demands and its demand for greater autonomy from the Central Government with regard to the Indian states. By creating Sant Bhindrawala, Mrs. Gandhi had all the political parties urging her to attack the Golden Temple. The notion of "Khalistan"[3] was supported and fostered by Mrs. Gandhi. One of the major advisors to Sant Bhindrawała was General Bhullar, who was sent to the United States to incite the Sikhs abroad. It was he who insisted that Khalistan be the goal of the World Sikh Organization. There is no question that every Sikh was hurt and angry after Mrs. Gandhi attacked the Golden Temple. I know for sure that there were some sincere but misguided Sikhs who fell right into her trap and took to violent struggle against the Indian government to demand a Sikh state. In fact, the leadership of the Khalistan movement did not have the interests of the Sikhs at heart nor did they have anything to do with Sikh spirituality.

Most of you know about Christ. Let me share with you very briefly what it means to be a Sikh. The Sikhs believe that the essence of all beings is the Creator we call Waheguru. Therefore, a Sikh who truly believes in the scriptures cannot discriminate against anyone on any grounds; race, creed, gender or belief system. What keeps us apart from each other and creates a sense of duality is our Haumain (roughly translated as ego)-- the "I" consciousness; i.e., "I am." The more "I am" attached to Haumain consciousness, the more I create distance between my self and others. The purpose of being a Sikh is to reduce Haumain consciousness and to enhance universal consciousness through loving devotion to Waheguru and to be in the service of its Creation. Any kind of discrimination among human beings is repudiated throughout the 1430 pages of Sri Guru Granth Sahib, the sacred Book of the Sikhs, their living Guru. This book includes the hymns of the saints from every religion or caste in India, and the Sikhs consider their hymns with the same reverence as they do the Sikh Gurus. For any Sikh to preach sectarianism is against the basic tenets of the Sikhs, as it is clear from the following quotes:

Ek Pita Ekas Ke Ham Barak

There is one Father and we are all His children

Guru Nanak

Tum Mat Pita Ham Barak Tere

---

3   The Sikh's demand for a separate country or homeland in Punjab.

You are our Mother and Father and we are your children

Guru Nanak

Manas Ki Jat Sabhe Ek Hi Pehchanbo

Recognize all human beings as one

Guru Gobind Singh
Dasam Granth P.26

For a Sikh to ask for anything but the Naam (Creator by any Name) is a distraction from the spiritual path.

Tudh Baj Hor Jo Mangna Sir Dukhan Ke Dukh Deh Naam Santokhia Utre Man Ki Bhukh

Asking for anything other than You is pain beyond any pain. Through the blessing of Your Name, I am contented and my mind is cleansed of all its appetites

For a Sikh to use religion for political gains is sacrilegious. After the massacre of Golden Temple, and then after the assassination of Indira Gandhi and the wholesale massacre of Sikhs all over India, wherever the Congress government was in power, the political leadership exploited the hurt and anger among the Sikhs to its own advantage. To control the Gurdwaras and use their income there was violence perpetrated by one or the other of the fighting Sikh factions. In Punjab, it resulted in total lawlessness perpetrated by politicians, drug smugglers, police and the so-called Sikh militants. It did not solve any of the problems confronting the people of Punjab. It has left the State totally bankrupt and in utter chaos.

We are seeing the ethnic cleansing that is occurring in Bosnia occupied lands by Israel and in other parts of the world. Since Hitler, we have created states in the name of religion and have brought untold suffering to the people concerned.

In July 1989, I was on a workshop panel on "The Tragedy of Violence, The Drama of Nonviolence." Dr. Khalid Siddiqui, the Director of the Islamic Education and Information Center, and Principal of the South Bay Islamic School in California, and Javed Ellahie, J.D. presented, "Islam: The Religion of Submission and Misconceptions Regarding Jihad." I was surprised to learn that Jihad has nothing to do with the idea of perpetrating violence against the non-Muslim Kafirs as perpetuated by the political leaders and the press. It has to do with conquering the eight impulses that distract humans from a righteous spiritual path. After a person has developed such self-control, he goes to Mecca for Hajj[4] to surrender himself to Allah in the service of humanity.

Fortunately, in India, the Muslims have begun to realize how they have been exploited by the religious and political elite, Ahamad et al (1992) in the October 31, 1992 issue of INDIA TODAY published a lead article describing this grass roots and widespread movement. Following are some excerpts:

For years we did what the Maulanas wanted. And see where they have landed us, now even they will not be able to stop us.

Sameena and Uzma Usmani
Engineering Students

A survey conducted in 1988-89 by the Planning Commission revealed that against the national literacy rate of 52.11%, the average for Muslims was 42%. The state of the women was abysmal. While the national female literacy figure was 39.42%, the corresponding figure for Muslim women was only 11%.

Muslim leaders had a vested interest in keeping the community in a quagmire so that they could continue to dominate them.

A, K. Akbar, Journalist

Mullahs are responsible for the state Muslims are in as they have vested interests. Only technical skills and self employment will help us get ahead.

Shabab Ali Khan
School dropout but the best
Car Mechanic

---

4   Pilgrimage

Most Punjabis understand the havoc caused by the politicians, smugglers, police and so called Sikh militants for their personal vested interests or ignorance. This is why, in spite of their best efforts and the violent intimidation waged against them, the Punjabis have not given in. In the United States, the politics of divisiveness worked in 1988, but the people rejected it in1992. Now Congressman Tom Campbell of California is trying to liberate the Republican Party from the Religious Right. One has to stand steadfastly against anyone who uses religion for political or material gains instead of focusing on the spiritual development of the individuals and service to humanity.

Racism and Scapegoating

Hitler used Jews as a scapegoat in a very masterful way. Racism was quite rampant in Europe in general and Germany in particular. On one hand, he glorified the Germans with such statements as the following:

> **What we must fight for is to safeguard the existence and reproduction of our race and our people, the substance of our children and the purity of our blood, the freedom and independence of the fatherland, so that our people may mature for the fulfillment of the mission allotted it by the Creator of the universe.**

Hitler, while analyzing all the ills of Germany and its defeat during World War I, placed all the blame on the Jews and implied that they rejoiced in the defeat of Germany and belittled their true leaders.

> **It required the whole bottomless falsehood of the Jews and their Marxist fighting organization to lay the blame for the collapse on that very man who, alone with superhuman energy and willpower, tried to prevent the catastrophe he foresaw and save the nation from its deepest humiliation and disgrace. By branding Ludendorff as guilty for the loss of the World War, they took the weapon of moral right from one dangerous accuser who could have risen against the traitors to the fatherland.**

Hitler exploited the jealousy against the financial success of the Jews:

> Finance and commerce have become his complete monopoly. His usurious rates of interest finally arouse resistance, the rest of his increasing effrontery indignation, his wealth envy...people begin to look at the foreigner more and more closely and discover more and more repulsive traits and characteristics in him until the cleft becomes unbridgeable. At times of the bitterest distress, fury against him finally breaks out, and the plundered and ruined masses begin to defend themselves against the scourge of God.

Has this kind of scapegoating stopped since Hitler? The Governor of California,

Mr. Pete Wilson attributed the decline of California's economy to foreign immigrants in spite of the fact that all of the studies show that immigrants are more of an asset rather than a drain on California's economy. Hitler promoted a kind of social Darwinism in glorifying the Aryan race over other races:

> Nature does that just by subjecting the weaker part to such severe living conditions that by them alone the number is limited, and by not permitting the remainder to increase promiscuously, but making a new and ruthless choice according to strength and health.

This kind of social Darwinism is still in vogue in some circles. Reviewing some of the quotes above, one may be misled that Hitler was an exception in being racist. In fact, racism is quite a universal phenomenon. It has been with us since the dawn of history and it is quite prevalent today. Michael Parenti (1992) traces the roots of racism to slavery and colonial imperialism. He defines racism in the following way:

> Racism is the belief and practice that treats ethnically distinct groups as biologically and morally inferior. ... In tribal times, the alien was not considered to be the moral equivalent to one's own people.

In the Western culture, Parenti went back to the founder of the intellectual tradition, Aristotle,

He quotes from POLITICS:

> Some men are slaves by nature and others are free men. By the condition of their soul some are inferior to others. This being so it is advantageous to both parties for that man to be a slave and that to be a master. It is good and just that some to govern and others to be governed in the manner that the nature intended.

Slavery became an institution during surplus accumulation of wealth. The Christian Church was one of the biggest slave owners. Therefore, the saints had to justify it with religious authority.

> Be dedicated to them who are your masters with fear and trembling as unto Christ.

St. Paul

> Slaves should not be set free at the public cost lest they become slaves of lust.

St. Ignatious

> Slavery is a path to servitude; the lower the status in life, the more exalted the Virtue.

St. Ambrose

Slaves were prohibited to enter the church. Saint Leo the First warns:

> The sacred ministry is polluted by such vile company and the rights of owners are violated.

During the 15th through the 18th Centuries, Christian missionaries developed relations with slave traders.

Twenty years ago, South Africa defended apartheid by quoting Genesis 918 and Joshua 921:

> Blacks were to be considered children of Ham.

In SWORD AND A DOLLAR, Michael Parenti makes a case that racism is also a result of imperialism. He paraphrased Thomas Morton who befriended the Native Americans, celebrating the great wonders of North America and praising the friendliness of the people.

Captain Mason

George Washington compared the red Indians to "wolves, both being the beasts of prey though they differ in shape."

Kaiser Wilhelm slaughtered 6,000 of an 8,000-member African tribe and called them baboons, In his poem "White Man's Burden " Rudyard Kipling refers to the Asian victims of British Imperialism as "half devil, half child."

Churchill judged Afghans as "dangerous and as sensible as mad dogs fit to be treated as such," and he recommended the use of poison gas.

Lloyd George, the Prime Minister of England, stated that his government should retain the right to kill "niggers." He was referring to Asians and Africans.

Justifying overseas expansions, numerous American presidents have talked about the "Anglo Saxon obligation to uplift and civilize supposedly inferior peoples," as McKinley said of Filipinos and as Woodrow Wilson said of all Latin America.

For us to externalize our racist tendencies and place them on one person such as Hitler is asking for a continuation of the same human destructive pattern.

Michael Parenti further quotes from Deuteronomy 232:

Moses tells us how Lord Jehovah lends a homicidal helping hand to its chosen people. The leader of an alien tribe and its army came to fight us, and our Lord delivered him to us. We smote him and his sons and all his people and we took all his cities at that time and utterly destroyed men and women and the little ones of every city. We let remain only the cattle we took as prey and the spoils of cities to ourselves.

In the East, the Brahmins were even smarter. They incorporated racism into the theory of creation. The Brahmins were created from the head of Brahma and their role was to attend to intellectual and spiritual pursuits. Kashtris were created through the arms of Brahma and they were the warriors, the ruling class. The Vaish were created from the belly of Brahma. They were the artisans, craftsmen, merchants and landowners. The Sudras were created from the feet of Brahma. Their job was to serve the other three castes and do all the menial jobs. These distinctions were enforced with the same kind of cruelty and rigidity as in Western civilization.

In looking at Hitler's hatred of the Jews, Erikson did an interesting analysis of the symbols of being a Jew and a German but he totally ignored the socioeconomic and political climate of Germany. Hitler hated the international stock market and the economic institutions, the politicians, the press and Marxism. He thought that Jews were in a dominant position in all these spheres and he even accused them of being the carriers of foreign ideas and of being responsible for Germany's downfall. To this day, the power elite has not stopped using the same scapegoating process of invoking racist images for political gains. I have already discussed how Indira Gandhi used Sikhs to further her political power. Former President Bush evoked racist images (Willy Horton) to win the election in 1988. The 1992 Republican Party platform is noteworthy for its exclusionary emphasis. You may say that no one was as cruel as Hitler, but such things as "ethnic cleansing" in Bosnia are going on today. The earlier quotes of justification for murder, genocide and for recommending poison gas are not exceptions, rather, almost every nation has a history of atrocities and, at time, genocide. In fact, all of us are racists to some degree. As long as we are attached to our ego, our country, and our culture in a way that requires us to prove that we are the chosen ones or the super race or the super power, or that requires that we have to fight for our selfish interest at the individual or national level, we will continue to be cruel and destructive toward our fellow human beings. There is nothing wrong in maintaining one's national or cultural identity, so long as we see it as a manageable unit of humanity that we can serve but not to see ourselves superior over others and exploit them for our own vested interest.

Economists have the very difficult task of developing an economic system based on cooperation and the common interest of humanity rather than on the vested interests of corporations or nations.

The Power Elite

The power elite in every country has very little interest in attending to the wellbeing of its own people. The power elite is comprised of the politicians, business leaders, press, religious leaders and educators. It is not an "us" versus "them" situation. All of us are members of this power elite in one way or the other. The only people who could be considered the victims of this power elite are petty criminals in jails, homeless people, and persons in mental hospitals. All of us but the most disenfranchised persons contribute in some way to the power elite. Following is a brief description of categories of the power elite.

Politicians

Politics is the art of manipulation of power and influence. No matter what form of government or socio-economic level of the country, the politicians use almost the same processes to acquire power and maintain it. Before I came to the United States in 1958, I lived in Punjab. The Sikh leaders would come to town and evoke a tremendous following by saying, "Khalsa ji Panth is in danger." (Respected members of the Sikh community, the Sikh community is in danger.) I used to think they were able to exploit the poor innocent farmers of the Punjab. Then, on coming to the U.S., I found that even in one of the most powerful, highly educated, and richest countries in the world the same ploys are used. President Reagan told us that U.S. security was threatened by Granada, and the people were proud of him that he restored America's honor through military intervention.

We have seen newsreels of how Hitler created an almost hypnotic trance in his followers by the display of German flags and the use of nationalist slogans. Have you seen displays that play on the emotions of national pride used since Hitler? The stage design of the Republican Convention of 1992 was very similar to Hitler's podium. We deplore Hitler's propaganda machine, yet have nations signed any agreement that such things are destructive and to be avoided? **We must focus on problem solving and on finding ways to better the lot of the people who are least able to represent their own interest.** On the other hand, we have refined the techniques of propaganda to a science. Today, politicians are not elected on their own merit and service record rather they are sold to the public like soap and cars by Madison Avenue.

Business Leaders

Since money is power and politics is an art of manipulation of power and influence, it is no surprise that they go together. Former President Bush's Century Club members (who donated more than $100,000 to his campaign) bought positions and influence with that money. The Gulf War was fought under the guise of national interest, but the only people who gained from that war were the oil companies and the banks, custodians of $100 billion dollars of Kuwait money. In the U.S. this war did not help employment and it could be seen to have contributed to more homelessness than at any other time in history. The Gulf War had nothing to do with justice or democracy or national interest. It only served the interests of the political and business elite. We are surprised when we see corruption at the highest level in every government, from President Bush's son, Neil Bush, to senators and congressmen. The political and business elite of 75 countries was involved in the corrupt practices of the Bank of Commerce and Credit International (BCCI). It could be more appropriately known as the Bank of Crooks and Criminals International. Such practices among the ruling class have always been prevalent. Now, sometimes they get caught.

The Press

The press is controlled by the ruling class in totalitarian regimes. In democratic countries, the press is controlled through intimidation. During the Gulf War, there was a total blackout of news. The CNN reporter who continued reporting from Baghdad was compared to Tokyo Rose. The press is, of course, owned by big money. The corporations that support the media through their advertisements have a powerful influence on what gets in the print, radio and television media. Now ABC is owned by Walt-Disney and NBC by G.E. Corporation.

Religious Elite

The clergy and organized religion, in general, have very little to do with the spiritual development of their people, Organized religion has been either self-serving or has been a handmaiden of the political powers which is discussed at length on Page 25.

Educational Elite

The beginning of all knowledge and learning has been metaphysi-
cal including human beings searching and exploring the mysteries of
nature and its relationship to us. There was a reverence and joy in living
in harmony with nature, as embodied in the various Native American
belief systems, in Shintoism, and in the pagan traditions of the West. But
at some point in human history, we discovered that knowledge is power.
It changed the course of modern education. So far, the basic motivation
of science has been to control and exploit nature and not to be a part of
it and live in harmony with it. For a detailed discussion of this, I would
refer the reader to "Reflections on Gender and Science" by Evelyn Fox
Keller (1985). She quoted Francis Bacon in her book;

> **'It is Nature herself who is to be the bride, who requires taming,
> shaping, and subduing by the scientific mind. I am come in very truth
> leading you to Nature with all her children to bind her to your service
> and make her your slave.'**

This is the same mentality that justified slavery, imperialism and racism.
It is no wonder that the universities themselves have become the cita-
del of promotion of self-interest and adversarial relationships. It is hard
to imagine that these universities will educate students in humanistic
values.

Conclusions and Recommendations

I have presented the view that it is not fruitful to scapegoat one individual for the destruction caused in the past. To prevent further destruction, we need to look at the pressures impinging on different units of
human organization and the structures and processes available to them
to resolve those pressures.

I have stated that the power elite in any country does not have the interest of its people at heart. It caters to the interests of itself, the power elite.
By this I do not mean to scapegoat the power elite. People do what they
can do and not even what they think should be done. Until now our
political process has been power based. Even M. K. Gandhi's passive
resistance was power based. Democracy is also power-based, and it has
not prevented human destruction. We have used power in most of our
human relationships because there was no alternative technology avail-

able, Now we have ample technology available to have non-power-based problem solving and conflict resolution. By now we have experienced that power-based conflict resolution never resolved any human problems. We may now be ready to try new methods. So far human civilization is based on Haumain and its extensions of greed, anger, sexual lust, pride and attachment. We need to try love and service as the future of human civilization is at stake. The foundation of non-power-based conflict resolution was developed in solving the intra-psychic conflicts of the individual through a psychotherapy process. This foundation was expanded in scope to family and then to organizational conflict resolution. The concepts of leadership and teaching are undergoing a revolutionary change. Our power elite is behind the times. President Clinton is starting with the emphasis of recognizing the problems and then going about solving them with the best possible technology and human resources available. My apprehensions are about how long this wonderful task focus of identifying and solving the problems will last. When we get stuck, we usually go back to our old ways. This is the time when a consultant should be called upon.

Metaphysical View

Human consciousness is constantly evolving. In spite of our harrowing experiences of past, I still believe that we continue to make progressive approximations toward a cosmic inter-connected consciousness. In this sense, I am a cynical optimist. We are going to get to our destination, not because of enlightenment but because of the high risks involved. When we look around and see what we have been doing to ourselves, our planet and our fellow human beings we see a very dismal picture. When we see where we came from it is very encouraging. We have evolved from a feudal system to city and national states and we are beginning to realize that we have no choice but to give up our old notions of short-sighted self-interest. We have to find unity in diversity and learn to live with it. We are one.

Liberation from the Power Elite: Liberation from Ourselves

We have seen national liberation from colonial powers. It is time to be liberated from our own power elite in each country that exploits its people for its own advantage. In other words it is time for liberation from our selves in terms of freedom from our own attachment to Haumain pursuits. Only then we will select leaders who will represent the humanistic values that all of us subscribe to and incorporate them in our selves. Freedom of information and scrutiny of the power elite by grass roots organizations will accomplish this task. This is taking place in many countries right now.

We must develop an equitable international economic system based on cooperation rather than the short-term vested interest of the power elite. This is the most difficult task. It is not easy to change an oppressive economic system. As an individual it is harder not to support an excessive consumption oriented economy. **The major responsibility falls on each of us to change the course of destruction.**

We must renounce violence to solve problems. In the history of humankind, violence has never solved a single problem. Violence is usually used to perpetuate self-interest and not to solve problems. Fortunately, there is fairly advanced technology available for conflict resolution and for productive problem solving. Former President Jimmy Carter's Mediation Center has made efforts in political conflict resolution. It is sad that so far, the United Nations still has an old fashioned approach to political problem solving through power manipulation and force instead of developing conflict management teams and making them available to disputing parties before they take to arms.

My personal experience is that the manifest problem defined by the conflicting parties is never the problem. It takes a lot of patience, skill and guts on the part of the consultant to go beyond the apparent conflict and discover a common ground. The new generation of politicians may be more receptive to actual problem solving and peaceful conflict resolution rather than rationalizing the wholesale massacre of people for a short-sighted self-interest or to gain political points to exploit the populace. We have to open our hearts and not let our intellect rationalize our most cruel and hideous acts, or to feel satisfied by singling out individuals and punishing them. We have to approach everyone with a loving heart and learn from our past experiences rather than evoke punitive value judgments on our selves and each other. We are the same and we are all in the same boat.

Question and Answer

Audience Participant: Dr. Singh you seem to be very idealistic and do not understand how economics works.

Singh: You are absolutely right. But, my question is not how economics works but how it does not work. It does not seem to be working if three fourths of humanity live in poverty and there are continuous wars to promote vested economic interest of a few in a community or a nation.

Post Script: 5-23-17

The above paper was presented in 1993.

Trump's election in 2016 illustrates all the points I made in the 1993 paper. Like Eric Erikson there are more than 100 mental health professionals who want to provide a psychiatric evaluation of Donald Trump. Yet, he is just a symptom of our dysfunctional system of modern civilization. It would be more productive to see the national socio-economic-political system that he represents if we want to develop an egalitarian democratic society and live in peace on this planet. Like many politicians before him, Donald Trump has done the following:

1. Exploited the frustrations of the dis-enfranchised segment of the population.

2. Has appealed to white supremacists (racism) to make America great again.

3. Invoked religious competition and scapegoating: Muslims hate us and Mexicans are criminals and rapists.

4. Promoted and protected the economic interests of the business and money lending class.

5. Supported privatization of education to continue the class system instead of promoting public education for all citizens and promotion of an egalitarian democratic society.

6. Attacked institutions necessary for a democratic society, such press, judiciary and congress.

7. Promoted violence against the opposition.

8. Made most of his cabinet appointments to promote his agenda and not the national or global humanitarian interest.

9. Told lies to placate his base.

10. Hitler said Jews celebrated Germany's defeat in World War I. Trump said that he saw thousands of Muslims celebrating Nine Eleven attack on World Trade Center (Absolutely false statements)

There is Hope Now: During Hitler's time people were easier to manipulate. From experience of the tragedies of the last century people have awakened. When President Trump signed the executive order against Muslim travellers, by the next morning millions of people took to the streets spontaneously to demonstrate against it. **The most important, hopeful aspect of these demonstrations was not to incorporate the values of hate and discrimination against Trump and his supporters. Banners showed that they were against bullying and hatred. The transgender people were dancing in the streets with love AND NOT HATRED. I hope we can maintain loving concern and avoid possession by hatred, self-righteousness and revenge. Otherwise we will continue destroying each other. We will just be taking turns to be on top in destruction of each other. Love thy enemy.**

The Commercial Press is owned by the corporations promoting Donald Trump's narrative representing the State Department and corporate interests rather than educating the public to create an informed citizenry necessary for a democratic society. Two days ago CNN was covering President Trump's visit to Saudi Arabia. When the King of Saudi Arabia was speaking, the press panelists did not listen to him and said that they are waiting for Donald Trump to speak. They kept talking among themselves. **How can we have a productive dialogue if we only listen to ourselves and not to others who have a stake in the wellbeing of this planet?**

After Donald Trump's speech they thought he was presidential and followed the script. He was talking about terrorism and defining the problem of terrorism in this world in terms of Muslim extremists. None of the panelists challenged his narrative. There are extremists in every community and every nation. They did not help develop a comprehensive understanding of the causes of terrorism. They followed the narrative of Donald Trump to scapegoat and externalize the blame to the Muslim community extremists. Leaving aside the state sponsored terrorism, more people are killed in the United States by white extremists than by Muslim extremists. Trump was beckoning the Muslim leadership in their countries to get rid of these terrorists and drive them out of their countries. What is he going to do with the non-Muslim terrorists in our United States?

President Trump was happy that he was able to persuade the Arab leaders to join Israel to fight the common enemy, Iran. He is happy to sell arms to promote the arms industry. Selling arms among nations will promote divisiveness not peace. One of the journalists said that Shias and Sunnis have been fighting for centuries. Actually, the Sunnis and Shias did not have any wars until the United States invaded Iraq, Libya and encouraged regime change in Syria by arming the opposition to the government. There is hardly any disagreement that ISIS is a direct result of our invasion of Iraq and Libya. There was no discussion of our foreign policy.

For details see Section V Intervention and Regime Change on Page 108 in Chapter II's Bibliography, which references United States' foreign policy.

References

Ahamad, F., Menon, R, and Ansari, J.M. (October 31, 1992). Young Muslims Forging a New Identity, New York: India Today.

Awasthi, D, and Ghimire, Y. (August 15, 1992), Politics of Opportunism. New York: India Today.

Caplan, G. (1964). Principles of Preventive Psychiatry, New York: Basic Books.

Erikson, E. H. (1963). The Legend of Hitler's Childhood in Childhood and Society. New York: W. W. Norton & Company.

Gupta, S., Basu, K, and Bose, F. (August 15, 1991). Cross Fire; Punjab, New York: India Today.

Hitler, A. (1925). Mein Kampf. Boston: The Houghton Mifflin Co.

Keller, E. F. (1985). Reflections on Gender and Science. New Haven: Yale University Press.

Menninger, K. (1966). The Crime of Punishment, New York: Viking.

Parenti, M. (October 1992). Racism from Aristotle to George Bush. Berkeley: KPFA Radio (924-109).

Singh, R. K. J., Chen, R. and Tarnower, W. (1971) Community Mental Health Consultation and Crisis Intervention. Palo Alto: National Press.

Singh, R. K. J. (1975). Beyond Camelot - Making Work A Growth Stimulating Situation. Paper presented at the National Convention of American Public Health Association at Chicago. Available at website: humanliberation-meji.com   Email: humanliberationmeji@gmail.com

Singh, R. K. J. (1989). My Practice: Interactional Consulting. Berkeley: Vision Action Vol.8,N0.4 December 1989, (23 through 25)

Chapter – II

DID INDIA AND PAKISTAN WIN FREEDOM?

In February 2017, Gurmehar Kaur, displayed the following banner in a demonstration at Delhi University

MY FATHER WAS NOT KILLED BY PAKISTAN

HE WAS KILLED BY WAR

This banner had created a national furor in India. There have been death threats and violent statements against her by the Bharatiya Janta Party (BJP) members and its political base Shiv Sena and Rashtariya Swayam Sewak Sang (R.S.S.S).

Her banner raises a simple question for each one of us:

Am I For Violence, Murder and Destruction caused by war?
or
Am I For Love, Peace and Prosperity?

This has been a perennial conflict and unanswered question throughout human history. There were persons who followed the path of love, peace and prosperity for all. The ruling elite of the time pursued their sectarian vested material interests and attacked, persecuted and murdered those persons who had followed the path for peace. For a **global one-humanity interest,** we need to resolve this perennial question for ourselves because our very survival depends on it.

Now instead of political furor we need to resolve this conflict within each one of us:

Am I for Moses who loved humanity and freed the slaves?
or
For the Pharaoh who tried to kill him and the slaves he had freed?

Am I for Christ who brought the message of love and wanted

us to even love those who consider us their enemies?

or

Am I for the Romans and Pharisees who
conspired to brutally murder him?

Am I for Muhammad who preached love of God and
equality of all humans; the slave and the master are equal?

or

The Mecca ruling elite who tried to murder him and
pursued him to Medina to kill him and his followers?

Am I for Mughal Emperor Aurangzeb who killed his brothers
to become Emperor of India and murdered Guru Tegh Bahadur?

or

For Guru Tegh Bahadur who beseeched Aurangzeb not
to kill innocent human beings only because they
worshipped the Creator differently than him?

Am I for the British Raj, Gandhi, Nehru and Jinnah who
caused genocide on both sides of the border of India and
Pakistan, with the murder of over one million persons and
forcing over eighteen million people to abandon their ancestral
homes and leave their neighbors and friends behind?

or

For those who were the victims of these leaders inability
to get along with each other and resolve conflicts peacefully,
leaving behind a perennial conflict between two peoples?

Did India and Pakistan Win Freedom?

A Collage of Explorations

Lessons Learned for Current Global Political Situation to Change the Course of Destruction

The following was written as a summary of my lifelong explorations
on this topic during the course of 2016-2017. I am calling this a collage
for two reasons. First it is not a linear narrative of India and Pakistan's

freedom. It brings in historical context, populace view and personal experience in addition to the political leaders. Secondly the course of destruction is not a single entity. It is reflected in violence and riots, wars, refugees, terrorism, nuclear arsenal, climate change, the gap between the rich and the poor, disease, racism, punitive and unfair justice system, unbridled pursuit of money for misconceived vested interest of a few caused by imperialism.

Political history of the world demonstrates that politics is the art of manipulation of power to one's best advantage. It really does not matter what kind of political system there is. Whether it is monarchy, dictatorship or democracy, people who come up on top are masters of the art of manipulation. The means they could use may include physical power and violence, salesmanship, propaganda, use of money, or creating organizations to support them; most often it is a combination of all of them and whatever else is at their disposal.

The dynamics of the processes used is also very similar. The latest example is the Presidential election in the United States. Even though Hillary Clinton appeared to be very different, both were fighting for power. Donald Trump used the underlying frustration of the persons who feel disenfranchised and addressed their issues, regardless of whether or not the solutions were realistic. He used scapegoating of groups of people to explain the current situation. These are not new methods. Most politicians have used these, including Hitler, who described these so eloquently in Mein Kampf (1925). Hillary Clinton used gender identity and the support of the establishment and destroyed her opponent Bernie Sanders in the primaries with establishment help and false propaganda. In addition to what we already knew, this was evident from the Wiki leaks disclosures of emails exchanged within the Democratic establishment. Donald Trump and Hillary Clinton tried to demonize each other. Instead of demonizing, we need to listen to each other patiently with love and compassion to develop a **deeper understanding** of the issues and of each other that would bring us closer. A good **journalist** can help achieve this if they try to "understand" in depth the issues raised by any political figure instead of just commenting on the statements they make or chasing the tweets of Donald Trump.

We are passengers in the same train of modern civilization that is running on a track of self-destruction. We need to understand the underlying structures and processes that propel it on this track in order to change the course of destruction. During the aftermath of election most of the discussion in the commercial press and the establishment was quite non-productive. Focus was misplaced on persons and superficial issues to divert attention from issues related to the wellbeing of people and the ones that threaten our very existence on this planet.

The media, multinational corporations and the Democratic and Republican establishment are not held accountable for their joint efforts to deprive people in the richest country in this world of health, education, work and general welfare. They have destroyed country after country and created misery in this world by misinforming and misleading the public (Bibliography Section VI – Interventions and Regime Change p. 106).

In 72 years since the end of World War II we have not been successful in disarmament and destroying the nuclear arsenal. At the United Nations on July 7th, 2017, 122 nations signed a treaty declaring the possession of nuclear arms as illegal. None of the nuclear powers signed this treaty. The leaders of these countries are leading us to destruction. If victims try to fight back they are called terrorists.

Journalists are mainly responsible for the divisiveness in this country in particular and in the world in general. Instead of giving news for people to make their independent judgment in support of an informed public, the media promotes points of view and indulges in propaganda to maintain their business interests. You can tell a person's political orientation knowing which news sources they use. There is not a single news outlet I can go to get objective and factual news without a spin.

Unfortunately history is written to glorify the ruling class and their conquests. There were celebrations of their conquests; the wealth, women and slaves they marched in victory parades. Promoted are the glories of their ruling the world through colonizing and the exploitation of subjugated people and their resources. **Howard Zinn's People's History of the United States (1980) is an exception.** I hope more people from different countries would write such history where they live.

The 1947 Partition of India determined the course of my life. **I could not understand how such a horrifying tragedy can happen and the people responsible for it are worshipped as international icons!** In my tiny and obscure life I have tried to understand, how we could treat each other in awful, cruel ways? My efforts to reduce suffering of a relatively small number of people in my professional practice as a psychologist gave me some ideas. It is hard to change the destructive paradigm of our modern civilization. I participate in world peace and inter-faith organizations with modest impact. The following collage is also an effort to share my experience and observations with you near the end of my life's journey. I will be very grateful to you if you could share with me what it brings up for you in the context of your life experience and thusly, begin a dialogue of understanding.

Naale Bulbul Ke Sunoo Aur Hama Tan Gosh Rahoon

Hamnawa Mein Bhi Koi Gul Hoon Keh Khamosh Rahoon

Listening to the lamentations of a Bulbul and me keeping quiet

O companion Am I a flower that I should stay silent?

Alama Iqbal, Shikwa 1911

Introduction

The purpose of this collage of perspectives is to explore the processes and role of political personalities during India's struggle for freedom from the British in a broader Indian historical context. Such perspectives may contribute toward understanding, help us to promote desirable changes for the future and initiate more productive structures and processes to help us reverse the course of destruction. As a **case example** I will describe India's struggle for freedom starting with 12th century. After describing historical events, I will describe the populace and my experience of the 1947 Partition of India. My perspective on history is very much influenced by my professional work as a community psychologist and as a Punjabi American born in a Sikh Family in India. (My birthplace is now located in Pakistan). I will end the collage by discussing the implications of India's struggle for independence upon current geopolitical problems and possibilities

The reality of any event is impacted by a multitude of factors and has very complex dimensions. Any linear description is unreal. This is why I am calling my effort to write about India's freedom struggle a collage. India's independence struggle did not begin by fighting against the British colonial power. I am sure freedom at different levels is a perpetual struggle for the human journey on this planet. I would also like to request the reader to pay attention to the underlying processes and institutions and not just the manifest content of the events or persons involved. Try to associate in your mind if there are any parallels in the history of the place where you grew up. That may help us understand if there is a commonality in the underlying dynamics of the historical systems of our civilization. This may help in working toward bringing about change in the dysfunctional paradigm or system of the modern civilization.

I

Sources of Oppression in the Twelfth Century India

Oppression by the Religious Institutions

Manusmritis were written before the birth of Christ. It is a very complex religious system. It described the four different functions of a human society as the manifestation of Brahma. Each segment of society had a different function to perform. It is in the eighth century that Adi-Shankra made them based on birth. He justified oppression of certain segments of Indian society by making these professional divisions based on birth as a result of their past life, Karma. According to his theory Brahma (God) created Brahmins from his head. Their job was to study scripture and perform all the religious rituals. Brahma created Kashtriyas from his arms. They were the warrior caste and became the ruling class. Vaish were created from his belly. They were the working caste. Shudras, commonly known in the West as untouchables, were created from the feet of Brahma. Their job was to serve the other three castes and do all the undesirable jobs, such as taking care of the feces and rubbish, taking care of the dead animals and making leather goods from the skin of dead animals. They were not allowed to read or hear scripture. If they dared to hear scripture, molten lead was poured into their ears so they could not hear again. If a Shudra's shadow fell on a Brahmin he had to take a bath to cleanse himself of the pollution created by their shadow. The Shudras could not use the same wells or touch the food of other castes. They lived in their own ghettoes apart from the rest of the village and endured atrocities and indignities too many to enumerate.

One could not get out of their caste they were born in. They were born into the caste because of their Karma in their past lives. This went on for centuries and in some ways still exists. Brahmins also exploited other castes by creating religious rituals for which people had to pay the Brahmins to perform the rituals to redeem their sins and transgressions.

Oppression by the Ruling Class:

India was not ruled as one country. There were small kingdoms governed by Rajas and Maharajas. Alexander "the Great" invaded in the third century before Christ. The Muslim invaders from Afghanistan, Iran and Turkey began invading India in the eighth century, mostly to plunder. But there were some Nizams, Sultans and Nawabs who settled in India and ruled small states on their own. How they treated their subjects varied but one thing was common: the people had very little say and owed total obedience to their rulers. In general the people were quite demoralized.

II

The Beginning of a Freedom Movement

Freedom from Oneself through
Personal Transformation

There were spiritual beings who questioned the inhumanity of existing religious and governing practices. This began in twelfth century with Baba Sheikh Farid, a Muslim Sufi Punjabi poet. He emphasized love for God and His Creation in Sri Guru Granth Sahib (SGGS, p. 488):

Dilon Muhabbat jinn Saee Sacheah

Jin Man Hore Mukh Hore Se Kandeh Kacheah

Those who love with their heart are the True ones

Those who have one thing in mind and

Have something else on their lips are the false ones.

Baba Sheikh Farid

By the fourteenth century there were numerous poet saints from different religions, from different castes and from different parts of India who emphasized that to be one with God is to love God. One does not need any intermediaries or religious rituals. One needs a **guide** who can show this path of love and cosmic spiritual unity. We have to treat everyone with love. God does not dwell in mosques and temples. God dwells in people's hearts and in His Creation one has to be loving and kind, serve people and preserve Creation.

Masjid Dha Deh Mandir Dha Deh

Dha Deh Joh Kujh Vehnda

Ik Bande Da Dil Na Dhaaveen

Rab Dillan Vich Rehnda

Tear down the mosque Tear down the Mandir

Tear down everything in sight

But do not break a person's heart

Because God dwells in hearts

Baba Buleh Shah

These poet saints began to question the way people were being treated by the priestly class and the rulers. They denounced the traditional renunciation of life and practice of celibacy. Since God lived within us we did not have to torture our body or deprive it of pleasure or go to the jungles to look for God.

Farida Jungle Jungle Kia Bhawen Van Kanda Moren

Vassi Rab Hialieh jungle Kia Dhoonden

O Farid why are you roaming around
in forests and breaking thorns

God lives within our hearts why are you looking for him in jungles

Baba Sheikh Farid

SGGS 1378

Nanak Satgur Bhatieh Puree Hoveh Jugat Khavundeaan

Hassundean Khalundean Pahnandean Viche Hoveh Mukt

Nanak, devotion to the True Guru (God)
one can realize that one can

Achieve salvation while enjoying eating,
laughing, playing and dressing.

Sri Guru Arjan Dev

SGGS 522

Baba Hoar Khana Khushi Khawar jit
Khadean Tan Peereh Man Mein Chaleh Vikar

Baba, that eating is bad that creates pain in
body and mind is occupied with bad thoughts.

Baba Guru Nanak

SGGS 16

Ghaal Khai Kichh Hathon Deh

Nanak Rah Pacheneh She

He who earns honest living through hard work

Shares with the needy Nanak he recognize the path
(of spiritual excellence)

Baba Guru Nanak

SGGS 1245

They emphasized the importance of honest work and leading a normal social life. Inevitably such practices and writings challenged the current order and provoked the wrath of Brahmins, Mullahs and other rulers alike. Bhagat Namdev from Maharashtra (Mumbai), who made his living by printing designs on cloth, was barred from entering the Hindu Temple. The Mullahs refused to perform the Muslim burial rights when Baba Buleh Shah died. The ruler Sikandar Lodhi wanted to punish Bhagat Kabir. He accused Bhagat Kabir of theft, even murder and sentenced him to death by being publically trampled over by an elephant. In spite of Mahawat's efforts the elephant would not walk over Bhagat Kabir. Instead he saluted him with his trunk. Ultimately Kabir's life was spared. Here is one of Bhagat Kabir's Dohas describing the equality of all human beings:

Awal Allah Noor Upaya Kudrat Ke Sabh Bandeh

Ek Noor Te Sabh Jagg Upjeah Kaun Bhaleh Ko Mandeh

First Allah created Light all humans are created by Nature

The whole world came into being from the same Light

Then who are good and who are bad?

SGGS 1349

At the time of the invasion of India in the early sixteenth century by Babar, the founder of the Mughal Empire in India, Baba Guru Nanak was roaming in Punjab and singing his divine poetry (Gurbani), bringing the message of spiritual unity of the universe – Ek Onkar. There is one Creator, **Naam (literally means Name, i.e., Creator by any name)** who manifests It self in Its Creation. **The purpose of spiritual practice is to realize the Creator within one self and perceive the Creator in everyone and everything.** The socio-political implications are obvious. If the essence of all of us is one Creator then any punitive value judgments and discrimination on any grounds is a result of "spiritual ignorance." The question arises, if spiritually we are all one, then why there is so much inequality, conflict and suffering in the world?

The individual embodied spirit is there to experience the world in that particular body. But we get attached to our body and lost in pursuing its desires. This individual sense is called **Haumain – "I am."**

Haumain Eha Jaat Hai Haumain Karam Kamaeh

Haumain's function is that it accumulates Karmah

Sri Guru Angad Dev

SGGS 466

Haumain creates Karma and accumulates life experience through our five senses, while satisfying our needs and the impulses aroused that are associated with these needs. The five impulses are Kaam (sexual desire), Krodh (anger), Lobh (greed), Moh (attachment) and Hankar (pride). These serve a positive purpose in order to experience our life. Yet, the more we get attached to our Haumain pursuits, the more we accumulate the debris of our Karma, the more we get alienated from our true spiritual self. We lose the sense of spiritual unity of the universe.

Haumain Deerag Roag Heh Daru Bhi Is Maaeh

Kirpa Kare Jeh Apni Taan Gur Ka Shabad Kamaeh

> Haumain is a disease of the worse kind
> but the cure is also within it
>
> If God is in Grace, a person practices
> Guru's Shabad (Divine Verses)

Sri Guru Angad Dev

SGGS 466

Sunia Muniah Man Keeta Bhao

Antar Gat Teerath Mal Naoh

> Listening to Guru's words
>
> Incorporating it within oneself
>
> Mind filled with love
>
> One takes an internal pilgrimage
>
> To cleanse oneself (Of Haumain attachment)

Baba Guru Nanak

SGGS 4

Haumain is sometimes translated as ego but this does not convey the real sense of the concept. **Haumain does not have any value judgment. It is the attachment to Haumain motivated pursuits and obtaining personal satisfaction at the expense of others that creates problems.**

In addition to Naam (the Creator and Its manifestation in Its Creation.)

and Haumain (I am) **the third most important concept is Hukam (Order).** The universe is run according to Divine Order.

Hukmai Andar Sabh Ko Baahir Hukam Na Koe

Nanak Hukmai Je Bujhe Taa Haumain Kahe Na Koai

Everything is in Divine Order there is nothing outside of it

Nanak, if one understands this then one does not
make Haumain claims (That I am the doer)

Baba Guru Nanak

SGGS 1

We are a part of this Divine Order. The causality of any event is too complex and multi-dimensional. **The more we think, "I am the doer and I am apart from the Divine order," the more we have a sense of the "other" and lose the sense of cosmic spiritual unity.** We pursue self-centered activities for personal benefit no matter how much suffering we cause to "others" who we perceive as separate from us. It is like bleeding one part of our body hoping to create strength in other parts of the body. **We dehumanize others for personal gain or for gain for the ones we identify as an extension of ourselves, such as my relatives, my community, my country, my religion and so on.**

The purpose of spiritual practice or freedom from oneself is to reduce Haumain attachment, realize the Creator within and perceive the Creator in everyone else.

Haumain Naavai Naal Virodh Hai

Doai Na Vaseh Ik Thai

Haumain has enmity with Naam (Creator)

Both cannot reside in the same place

Guru Amar Das

SGGS 560

Jab Ham Hoteh Tab Tum Naahi

Abb Tum Ho Hum Naahi

When "I" was then You were not

Now that You are "I" am not

> Bhagat Kabir
>
> SGGS 339

Bisar Gaee Sabh Taat Praaee Jab Te Sadh Sangat Mohe Paaee

Na Ko Bairi Nahin Bigaana Sagal Sang Hum Ko Ban Aaee

......

Sabh Meh Rav Reha Prabh Ekai Pekh Pekh Nanak Bigsaaee

I have lost the jealousy and sense of otherness

Since I found the company of saints

Foe and stranger there is none

I am at peace with every one

......

Perceiving Creator in everyone

Nanak is in an eternal state of bliss

> Guru Arjan Dev
>
> SGGS 1299

A Farsi poet Shams Tabrizi described the same spiritual state in the following couplet:

Al Yak Charagh Masjid-o- But Khana Roshan Ast

Dar Cheeztam Dushmni Kufaro Deen Ast

One candle lights the same mosque and the idol house

Then why is there enmity between the Muslim and Kafir!

An Urdu poet Maulana Altaf Husssain Hali also expresses the same spiritual attainment as follows:

Us Hee Ke Noor Sai Mojoud Hai Sab Mein Noor

Shamah Haram mein Ho Diya Somnath Ka

It is the same Light that manifests It self everywhere

Whether it is a candle in Mecca or a lamp in Somnath Temple

III

Struggle for Freedom from the External Oppression

The period from sixteenth century to the middle of nineteenth century before the British entered Punjab is a fascinating period. During this time the spiritual movement referred to above reached its climax and was able to bring down the Mughal Empire. It is like a Divine Politico-spiritual play. I am going to introduce to you the characters of the play. When I present the modern struggle spanning the second half of the nineteenth century to the middle of the twentieth century of freedom from the British, I will introduce the characters of that time. You may be able to compare those characters with the characters involved during India's struggle for freedom from the British rule. The following characters were involved in two centuries of struggle and we will see the impact of this struggle in the nineteenth and twentieth century:

Baba Guru Nanak was born in Punjab in 1469. He was the second most travelled person in history at that time. He travelled to very sacred places. He went to Mecca, Sri lanka, Tibet and all over India. During his travels he not only had discourse with fellow spiritual beings, he also collected their writings. These were included in Sri Guru Granth Sahib by his fifth manifestation Sri Guru Arjan Dev ji in 1604. The ten Gurus listed below were his successors.

Babar was a Mongol who came from Central Asia and invaded India in 1525 and established a Mughal Empire in India. The seven emperors listed below were his successors who ruled India.

The Sikh Gurus   **The Mughal Emperors**

1. Baba Guru Nanak, 1469-1539 AD 1. Emperor Babar invaded India in

1525 A.D

2. Guru Angad Dev 1539-1552	2. Emperor Humayun, 1531–1540 1555–1556
3. Guru Amar Das 1552-1574	3. Emperor Akbar 1556-1605
4. Guru Ram Das 1574-1581	4. Emperor Jahangir 1605-1627
5. Guru Arjan Dev 1581-1606	5. Emperor Shah Jahan 1628-1658
6. Guru Hargobind 1606-1644	6. Emperor Aurangzeb 1658-1707
7. Guru Har Rai 1644-1661	7. Emperor Bahadur Shah 1707-12

8. Guru Harkishan 1661-1664

9. Guru Tegh Bahadur 1664-1675

10. Guru Gobind Singh 1675-1708

11. Sri Gur Granth Sahib: The sacred Book compiled by Sri Guru Arjan Dev (1704)

Guru Gobind Singh proclaimed it as the living Guru 1708-Present

When Babar invaded India, Baba Guru Nanak wrote verses on divine love and described the misery his invasion caused for the people:

Paap Ki Janj Lai Kablon Dhaaia Jory Mangai Daan Ve Lalo

Oh Lalo, Babar rushed from Kabul
with a marriage party of misdeeds

And was asking for offerings by force

Baba Guru Nanak

SGGS 722

Describing the murderous scene and suffering caused by Babar's invasion Baba Guru Nanak (SGGS 417) expressed:

Jin Sir Sohan Pattian Maangee Pai Sandhoor

Se Sir Kaati Munnian Gal vich Aweh Dhoor

The heads that supported beautiful hair

Had vermillion in the parting of their hair

Those hair were shaved with scissors and

The heads were rolling around in dust

Baba Guru Nanak (SGGS 145) spoke truth to cruel power and wrote about the ruling class of the time:

Kal Kati Raje Kasai Dharam Pankh Kar Ud Reha

The rulers of Dark Age are like butchers

Goodness has taken wings and flown away

In the dark night of falsehood

I espy not the moon of Truth anywhere

I grope after Truth and am bewildered

I See no path in darkness

It is the obstinacy with which

Man clings to his petty Haumain

That causes this anguish

Nanak asks where is the path of salvation

Baba Guru Nanak was imprisoned during this invasion. By this time he, along with other Bhagats and Pirs, had created a sense of cosmic spiritual unity among the Indian masses. He was well known and was loved by both Muslims and Hindus alike. He was known as

Nanak Shah Fakir

Hindu Ka Guru Muslim Ka Pir

Nanak Shah spiritual being

Is Hindu's Guru and Muslim's Pir

The greatest Urdu poet of the twentieth century Allama Iqbal wrote a poem called Nanak in his book Bang-e-Dara:

Phir Uthee Aakhir Sada Tauhidd Ki Punjab Se

Hind Ko Ik Mard-e- Kamal Ne Jagaya Khwab Se

Then arose a voice of spiritual unity from Punjab

A perfect man awakened India from the dream

When Babar came to know that Baba Guru Nanak was imprisoned he went to see him and asked for his blessings. Baba Guru Nanak told him that his rule would be sustained as long as he ruled with justice and was kind to his subjects.

Babar's son Humayun succeeded him. In the battle of Panipat, Sher Shah Suri defeated him. Humayun escaped to Punjab and went to Baba Guru Nanak's house where Guru Angad Dev ji had succeeded him. When Humayon reached there Guru Angad Dev ji was teaching young children and did not pay him any special attention. Humayun took it as an insult and drew his sword. Guru Angad Dev ji said that this sword would have been better used in Panipat instead of drawing it against Fakirs (holy men). Like his father Babar, he asked for forgiveness and blessings. Guru Angad Dev ji gave him the same blessings; that he would be victorious if he vowed to rule with justice and be kind to his subjects. Humayun did regain his throne.

There had been an ongoing relationship between the Gurus and Mughal Emperors. Akbar the Great came to visit the third Guru, Sri Guru Amar Das ji. The Gurus had institutionalized serving Langar (Meals for the congregation and the needy) from the time of Baba Guru Nanak. Everyone had to share a meal sitting as an **equal** with members of the congregation known as Pangat. People sat together regardless of their caste, creed or social status. Akbar the Great also did partake in Langar, sitting with everyone else before having an audience with the Guru. Before he departed he wanted to give the Guru a land grant. Guru ji told him that Gurdwara belongs to the people, that they support it and arrange Langar for all visitors and the needy. Then Akabr pledged the land grant to Guru Amardas's daughter as a Shagan (an affectionate gift with blessings from an elder) and deeded the land in her name.

Emperor Akbar had made efforts to unify India as a nation. He started Din-i-Illahi, his own version of a religion. This was opposed by the Mullahs. He also created the Urdu language, which had Hindi grammar and words from Farsi, Arabic and Indian languages. Urdu literally means army. The purpose was to have a language that all Indians could understand. His son Jahangir was not so open-minded. He did not have a very loving relationship with his father. Intense conflict developed between Emperor Akbar and his son Jahangir. Jahangir opposed his father's efforts for creating unity. He also became concerned about the popularity of the Gurus.

During Jahangir's time, Guru Arjan Dev ji, the fifth manifestation of Baba Guru Nanak, compiled the sacred book Sri Guru Granth Sahib. This book contains the verses from six Gurus and 29 saints, Bhagats and Sufis from different parts of India, writing in different Indian languages and representing different religions, castes, class and social status. In some sense it embodies the cosmic spiritual unity created by the saints, Bhagats and Sufis in India. **It was to recognize that love is the common thread that creates spiritual unity in all spiritual paths if you separate out the rituals that are artifacts of history and cultural influence of the time and place.** Many times rituals were created in the vested interests of Haumain driven individuals.

Guru Arjan Dev ji decided to build Harmandir, also known as Durbar Sahib and the Golden Temple, to enshrine the Sacred Book Sri Guru Granth Sahib, reflecting the spiritual unity of the universe. He invited his lifelong friend Sain Mian Meer, a Muslim Sufi saint, to lay the foundation stone of this shrine. Later, Maharja Ranjit Singh adorned the shrine with 24-carat gold plates. In the West it is known as the Golden Temple.

Emperor Jahangir became quite concerned about the nationwide popularity of the Gurus. He wrote in his autobiography, Tuzk-e-Jahangiri, that Guru Arjan was preaching falsehood. There were even Muslims who became his followers. This had to be stopped and the Guru had to be converted to Islam. There were some historical excuses found to arrest Guru Arjan Dev ji and he was tortured to death. He was made to sit on a hot griddle and hot sand was poured over him. At that time Sain Mian Meer came to see the Guru and pleaded him to approach Jahangir to seek to persuade him to stop this atrocious act. Guru Arjan Dev ji asked his friend to close his eyes and see through his spiritual eye. **Sain Mian**

Meer saw that the person who was pouring hot sand and the one sitting on the hot griddle were one and the same.

When his son Guru Hargobind ji was being initiated as the Guru by Bhai Budha ji, the Guru requested that he wear two swords; one for Piri (spirituality) and the other for Miri (temporal power). Until the fifth Guru the emphasis was on Bhakti, spiritual loving devotion to the Creator and social reforms. Guru Hargobind ji combined Bhakti (spiritual loving devotion) with Shakti (power). The Sikhs call their sword Kirpan, which means blessing or mercy. He advised his Sikhs never to use Kirpan in anger, or for revenge or in hatred. It was only to be used to protect the unprotected and to fight against injustice and oppression. He asked his followers to bring horses and weapons as offerings. He started training his Sikhs (Students) in martial arts. He fought four battles with the Suba Lahore (Mughal Governor of Lahore). **Until his time the Gurus raised the consciousness of people to incorporate within themselves the socio-spiritual values. With Guru Hargobind ji it became an open struggle to fight against injustice and oppression.** He invited ballad singers who sang the ballads of great warriors and their valor to inspire his **Saint Soldiers.**

Guru Hargobind ji was imprisoned by Jahangir in Gwaliar Fort with 52 other Rajas as political prisoners. Many of Jahangir's advisors held Gurus in high esteem. Sain Mian Meer was one of them. They prevailed upon him that Guru ji had no political ambitions. Jahangir ordered Guru ji's release. Guru ji demanded that unless all the political prisoners in Gwaliar Fort were released he would not leave. Emperor Jahangir ordered that anyone who could hold on to his robe would be released. Guru ji ordered a robe with fifty-two corners. Each Raja could hold on to one corner. Thus all the fifty-two Rajas were freed. The Guru began to be known as Bandi Chhor (the Liberator).

After his release, Jahangir had him as his guest and companion. It is told that once on a hunting expedition Guru ji saved the life of the emperor by intercepting and killing a lion that had leaped at the emperor from nowhere.

Guru Har Rai had an armed force with him but he spent most of his efforts in running a hospital and preserving nature by planting trees, herbs and flowers. He saved Jahangir's life by providing his Vaid (Physician) with the required herbs when Jahangir was seriously ill.

Aurangzeb established himself as the Mughal Emperor after killing three of his brothers and imprisoning his father, Emperor Shajahan (who built the Taj Mahal). A rule of terror fell upon India. Aurangzeb was a very pious man. He took no money from his royal treasury. Instead he made his living by copying Quran Sharif and selling them. He developed a great passion to save the soul of his non-Muslim subjects by converting them to Islam. Kashmir was a center of great learning in Hinduism. He told the Pundits that either they embrace Islam or they would be put to sword. Pundit Kirpa Ram brought a delegation of Brahmans to Anandpur Sahib, Punjab where lived Sri Guru Tegh Bahadur ji (the ninth manifestation of Baba Guru Nanak) and told him their tragic tale. Pundit Kirpa Ram's ancestors were Baba Guru Nanak's Sikhs. Later on Pundit Kirpa Ram became an Amrit Dhari Sikh named Sardar Kirpa Singh and joined the Khalsa Army. He was killed in the battle of Chamkaur Sahib.

The tragic story of the Brahmins from Kashmir created a sad pandemonium. Sri Guru Tegh Bahdur's nine-year old son, Gobind Rai asked why everyone was so sad. He was told about the suffering of the Brahmins from Kashmir. He inquired of his father for a solution to their suffering. Sri Guru Tegh Bahadur ji replied a sacrifice would be required of a great spiritual being. The son asked the father, "Who is greater than you?" (because he was the Guru). Guru Tegh Bahadur embraced him and sent a message to Emperor Aurangzeb, that if the emperor could convert him, all of India would be converted to Islam. Guru Tegh Bahdur travelled to Delhi along with three of his Sikhs. The emperor ordered their public execution in front of the Red Fort. One of the Sikhs was boiled alive and the other one was sawed from head to toe. On the third day Sri Guru Tegh Bahadur was beheaded. He is known as:

Gur Tegh Bahadur Hind Di Chaddar

Guru Tegh Bahadur is the Protective Sheet of India.

Now there is a Gurdwara Sis Ganj at this place in Delhi to commemorate Sri Guru Tegh Bahadur's martyrdom. This sacrifice was made to achieve freedom of worship according to one's own beliefs and religion.

At night a merchant, Lakhi Shah Vanjara, stole the body and concealed it in his merchandise in a wagon. He took the body to his house and set the house on fire to cremate the body. Now there is Gurdwara Rakab

Ganj in New Delhi. Bhai Jaita took the head to Anand Pur Sahib where it was cremated. His son Gobind Rai was told that Aurangzeb announced that if any one believed like Guru Tegh Bahadur he could claim his body. Nobody stepped forward. Gobind Rai, who created the Khalsa Army, said that he would give his Sikhs the courage of their convictions. Also, with their distinct appearance that he prescribed, they would be unable to deny what they stand for.

Guru Gobind Rai continued the martial arts training started by the sixth Guru Sri Guru Hargobind ji but on a very large scale. He built four forts in Anandpur Sahib. He asked the Pahari Hindu Rajas to join him in the fight against the cruelty and oppression of Emperor Aurangzeb. They refused to join him because his Sikhs did not practice a caste system. The Rajas were Kashtryas and they did not want to mix with the non-Kashtryas. If Guru Gobind Rai would create a separate Kashtrya force, the Rajas said they might consider joining him. Guru ji refused.

The Pahari Rajas began to fear Guru Gobind Rai with his fort building and well-trained army. The Guru ji was invited to attend the wedding of one of the Raja's sons and the Rajas decided to attack him because he had only a few hundred Sikhs with him on that occasion. A Muslim Sufi, Pir Budhu Shah, heard of this plan and joined Guru Gobind Rai with over 600 of his followers. That was the battle at Bhangani. Pir Budhu Shah's two sons were killed along with many of his followers. The Sikhs celebrated their victory over the Rajas' armies. Guru Gobind Rai told them it was not their victory as the Khalsa belonged to Waheguru, so the victory also belonged to Waheguru. The word Khalsa was used since Guru Gobind Singh abolished Masands and established the direct link between the Guru and his Sikhs.

On a Baisakhi festival day, March 30, 1699, Guru Gobind Rai ji sent messages to Sikhs all over India to come and receive a special boon created by the Guru. In spite of the Mughal check points, 80,000 Sikhs arrived in Anand Pur Sahib **from all over India.** After Asa Di Var Kirtan Guru ji drew his sword and asked if someone would be willing to sacrifice himself, **Bhai Daya Ram, a Khatri from Lahore,** stood up. Guru ji took him into a nearby tent, returned with a blood-drenched sword and asked for another person who would be willing to sacrifice himself. **Bhai Dharam Das, a Jat from Hastinapur (Delhi),** offered himself. The third person to offer self-sacrifice was **Bhai Mohkam Chand, a washer**

man from Dwarka. Then a fourth and fifth came forward; **Bhai Sahib Chand, a barber from Bidar,** and **Bhai Himmat Rai, a Jheever (water carrier) from Jagannath Puri.** The Guru brought all five of them (now known as the **Five Beloved Ones**) out of the tent. These five persons represented different castes and regions of India. They were dressed in blue robes, turban, shorts and wearing a sword. To initiate them on the Khalsa Path (Panth) he created a spiritual ceremony. He poured water into a steel bowl and asked one of the Sikhs to get sugar Pataseh (chips) from Mata Sahib Kaur. He stirred water and these Pataseh with a two edged sword while reciting five Banis. At the end he uttered Waheguru, sprinkled nectar on their heads and faces and invited each of the five Beloved Ones to drink this Amrit (Nectar). At the end of the ceremony of giving Amrit to the five Beloved Ones he kneeled before them and requested them to bless him with the boon of the Amrit. Bhai Gurdas Dooja (second) wrote about Guru Gobind Singh in his Var 41, published by SGPC:

Wah Prgatia Ik Marad Agamra Waryam Ikela

Wah Wah Gobind Singh Aape Gur Chelaa.

There appeared a unique warrior man who has no match

Praise Guru Gobind Singh himself is the Guru and Disciple.

To abolish their former caste identity, Guru Gobind Rai proclaimed that all Amrit Dhari males would have their last name as Singh, which means a lion and all Amritdhari women would have their last name as Kaur, meaning princess. Since he was also initiated by the five Beloved Ones as an Amritdhari Sikh, his name was also changed from Gobind Rai to Gobind Singh.

Gobind Singh proclaimed Khalsa as Akal Purkh's (Eternal Being) army and that:

Akal Purkh, Satgur Sabhna Da Bhala Manainda

The Creator wishes the wellbeing of all.

As a part of their Khalsa identity, the Guru prescribed a uniform with five distinguishing characteristics: 1. Kesh (unshorn hair) and a turban to cover them. 2. Kangha (a wooden comb) for hair care. 3. Kachera (knee length shorts) 4. Kara (a steel bracelet) and 5. Kirpan (sword). Remember that Kirpan is derived from word Kirpa meaning mercy or blessing. The Sikh sword is a Kirpan that is merciful. The army was to recite the five Banis every day to maintain their spiritual practice to prevent attachment to Haumain and live in cosmic spiritual unity. **They were to be self-less warriors to protect the unprotected and fight against injustice and oppression.**

The five Beloved Ones represented different parts of the country and different castes. This demonstrated Sri Guru Gobind Singh ji's intention to create an integrated national, humanistic army that was devoted to protect the unprotected and fight against injustice and tyranny. They were not fighting for any sectarian cause. Sometimes Sikhs minimize their sacrifices by using words for Khalsa Panth or for Sikh religious places. Their message is to fight against oppression. It happened to be in India but Khalsa fights for all humanity. Twenty thousand Sikhs became Amritdhari Khalsa warriors on that Vaisakhi day.

The Khalsa army fought against the oppressors and provided selfless service. They helped rescue women who had been abducted by ruthless members of the ruling class and returned them to their families. Battles were fought against Subedar of Lahore and local Rajas. The Khalsa army prevailed. Ultimately in 1704, all of the Pahari Rajas and Subedar of Sirhand, with the backing of Emperor Aurangzeb, attacked Anandpur Sahib. They could not break through the defenses of the forts. The Mughal and Raja's armies surrounded the forts and stopped any traffic from geting in and out of the forts for six months to no avail. Ultimately, the Raja's swore by their Gods and upon the honor of the Sacred Cow and Aurangzeb assured Guru Gobind Singh ji, swearing by Quran Sharif, that they would provide them safe passage if they vacated Anandpur Sahib. Guru Gobind Singh ji agreed. As soon as the Khalsa Army vacated the fort, the Mughal and Hindu Rajas attacked them.

The Khalsa fought their way across the flooded Sirsa River. Then Guru Gobind Singh ji's mother Mata Gujri ji, along with Guru Gobind Singh ji's two younger sons Baba Fateh Singh and Baba Zorawar Singh, went separately with their caretaker Gangu.

The Khalsa had the populace support of Hindus and Muslims alike. During the crossing of the Sirsa River, one of Guru Gobind Singh ji's distinguished warriors Bachitar Singh (1664-1705), son of Bhai Mani Singh, was badly injured. He stayed in the fort of Nihang Khan near Ropar while the rest of the Sikhs accompanied Guru Gobind Singh toward Chamkaur Sahib. Chaudhuri Jaffar Ali Khan of Ropar was informed that some of the Sikh soldiers were staying in in Nihang Khan's fort. He searched the fort but found no Khalsa soldiers until they reached one particular room. Nihang Khan told them his daughter Mumtaz was with her newly wedded husband. After the soldiers left Nawab's daughter Mumtaz tended to Sardar Bachitar Singh's wounds but he passed away. She never married and spent her life in selfless service. (This account is based on the narrative described online at tapoban.org.us.)

Guru Gobind Singh ji with forty Khalsa warriors, including two of his older sons, nineteen year old Baba Ajit Singh ji and seventeen year old Baba Jhujar Singh ji, reached Chamkaur Sahib and resided in a Hindu Rajput's Haveli. Ten thousand Mughal and Hindu Raja army soldiers surrounded the Haveli. They tried to overrun the Haveli but did not succeed. Guru Gobind Singh ji took the offensive. He sent a Jatha (a group of five Sikhs) to attack the army and provided them protection by showering arrows upon the enemy from the Haveli. Both of his sons also lead a Jatha. Each died fighting. In this way they kept the enemy at bay during the day. At night five Sikhs went to Guru Gobind Singh ji and beseeched him to leave the Haveli for his safety. They argued that he could then continue to raise the army and fight the Mughals.

Guru Gobind Singh ji escaped to the Machivara jungle. The Mughal army, in hot pursuit, had checkpoints all around Machiwara. Two Muslim brothers, Nabi Khan and Ghani Khan, who used to sell horses to Guru Gobind Singh ji and three Beloved Ones warriors helped Guru Gobind Singh jj escape by telling the checkpoint soldiers that Guru ji was Uch Da Pir (a Muslim holy man).

Guru ji travelled North in Punjab and reached Raikot where the Muslim Nawab of Raikot hosted him. It is at this point Guru Gobind Singh ji received the news that Gangu had betrayed the family for reward money from Subedar of Sirhand Wazir Khan. Suba Sirhand had announced that he would release Mata Gujri ji and Guru Gobind Singh Ij's two sons (nine year old Baba Fateh Singh and seven year old Baba Jhujar Singh) if Guru Gobind Singh ji would surrender. Receiving no response, he decided to murder the two children by having them buried alive in a wall.

He repeatedly asked them to accept Islam with the promise of all the honors and life as princes. The children refused.

At that time the Nawab of Malerkotla stopped in Sirhand on his way from Delhi to Malerkotla. He reminded Suba Sirhand that it was against Islamic law to kill innocent children and women. Suba Sirhand retorted that they were the sons of the enemy Guru Gobind Singh, who had killed Nawab of Malerkotla's brother in the battle of Chamkaur Sahhib. The Nawab replied that his brother was killed while fighting and his death could only be avenged in a fight, not killing innocent children. He walked out of the Durbar as a protest and Suba Sirhand carried out his sentence.

It is noteworthy that Sikhs never forgot this gesture of Nawab of Malerkotla. During the partition of India in 1947 when there was a complete genocide of Muslims in Punjab India and of Hindus and Sikhs in Pakistan, the Sikhs protected the Nawab and all the residents of his state; the majority of them were Muslims.

From Raikot, Guru Gobind Singh ji proceeded toward the river Bias. From there he proceeded to join Mai Bhago and her Jathas who were fighting the Mughal army. Now it is known as Muktsar. After defeating the Mughals at Mukatsar he stayed in Dina Kangar. This is where he wrote his famous Zafar Nama (Letter of Victory) in Farsi poetry to Aurangzeb. He started by describing what it means to be a Muslim and that Emperor Aurangzeb had failed to act like a Muslim. He described all the atrocities Aurangzeb had perpetrated while being unable to defeat the spirit of Khalsa. He invited Aurangzeb to visit him so that they could talk to each other. It is said after Aurangzeb received the Zafar Nama he wanted to visit Guru ji. Unfortunately, he died soon after. At Dam Dama Sahib Guru ji dictated Sri Guru Granth Sahib to Bhai Mani Singh and included the ninth Guru Sri Guru Tegh Bahadur's Bani. He remained there for nine months.

After Aurangzeb's death there was a power struggle for the throne of Delhi. Guru Gobind Singh ji, because he considered Bahadur Shah to be the rightful heir, helped him to capture the throne of Delhi. At his coronation he gave Guru Gobind Singh ji a Khillat (a royal token of apprciation). From Delhi, Bahadur Shah and Guru ji travelled towards the South. Guru ji decided to stay in Nander, now known as Hazoor Sahib, in Hydrabad Deccan. At Nander he met an ascetic, Madho Das

Bairagi, who was a great hunter and a warrior from Kashmir. He had turned ascetic because once he killed a pregnant deer that touched him deeply. He received Amrit from Guru Gobind Singh ji and was given the name of Banda Singh Bahadur. Guru ji chose him to lead an expedition to finish the Mughal Raj in Punjab. He organized and trained the Punjabi army that had Hindus and Muslims as a part of his Khalsa Fauj. He conquered Sirhand and went north to Gurdaspur District. During the short time that he controlled certain areas in Punjab he distributed the land to those farmers who were willing to till the land. Banda Singh was captured by Mughal armies in 1716. He, along with seven hundred other Khalsa soldiers, were paraded in Delhi and tortured to death.

After Banda Singh Bahadur's death, the Khalsa organized itself in twelve different Misls. These Misls had control over different parts of Punjab as well as areas across Yamuna River. Twice they captured Delhi Red Fort and left it with the ruler after he promised to take better care of the religious shrines and rule with fairness. During the nine invasions of India by invader Ahmed Shah Abdali (1747-1769) the Khalsa warriors would rescue the women who had been captured as slaves and returned them to their homes. All the wealth and treasures that had been looted in Delhi were re-captured and were used for the service of the people. There were two attempts at genocide of the Khalsa but the Khalsa would reappear with greater strength. Ultimately Suba Lahore wanted to make peace with the Khalsa. He offered a land grant with a title of a Nawab. **The Khalsa Sardars like Jassa Singh Ahluwalia were not fighting for any personal material rewards. They could make peace if the Mughals would stop their atrocities.** They offered the land grant and the title of Nawab to the person who was taking care of the horses.

The Misls continued until Maharaja Ranjit Singh subdued all the Misls by persuasion or conquest and established a kingdom near the end of the nineteenth century. His kingdom extended up to Khyber Pass Northwestern Frontier Province, to Kashmir and Tibet. In 1809 British Envoy Charles T. Metcalfe signed a treaty at Amritsar that they would not cross Sutlej river to the North and Maharaja Ranjit Singh will not cross into the territories South of Sutlej.

 Sikhs have tried to describe Maharaja Ranjit Singh's rule in sectarian terms as Khalsa Raj. It minimizes the true achievement. **It was truly the rule of the native sons of Punjab in the tradition of spiritual**

unity that India had achieved in the previous six hundred years. It was truly a humanistic administration. The Maharaja was a Sikh. The Chief Counsel and Foreign Minister was a Muslim Fakir, Aziz-ud-Din. The Prime Minister was a Dogra Hindu from Kashmir. They had great Sikh Generals like Hari Singh Nalwa and Akali Phula Singh along with other Generals who were Muslims, Hindus, Italians and French and even an American who had served in the Punjab Army. Ghaus Moham-mad Khan (Mian Ghausa) was in charge of the heavy artillery. Dewan Mohkam Chand was entrusted with the administration of Dallewalia Estates. He captured Pathankot and then proceeded to Jasrota, Chamba and Basoli and compelled the Raja to acknowledge the sovereignty of the Maharaja of Punjab. Over fifty per cent of the Khalsa Army was com-prised of non-Sikh warriors. There is consensus among historians that it was the most just and humanistic rule. There was no death penalty nor were there revengeful killings. This was no small achievement in that period of human history.

Maharaja Ranjit Singh died in 1839. After his death his oldest son Ma-haraja Kharak Singh was assassinated. After his funeral, when Prince Naunihal Singh was returning to his palace, he was also assassinated. The only successor to the Punjab throne left was Prince Daleep Singh, who was only five years old. The British, who had been creating their empire in the rest of India for a century, attacked Punjab. They made an arrangement with the Prime minister of Punjab Dogra Dhian Singh, who was originally from Kashmir. They promised to sell Kashmir to him if he would betray the Punjab's armies. He complied. Dhian Singh's fam-ily ruled Kashmir until 1947. There were two wars, 1845-46 and 1848-1849, between the Punjab Khalsa Army and the rest of British Indian army.

A Muslim Punjabi poet Shah Muhammad (1780/82-1862) wrote the ballad Kissa Shah Muhammad describing the Punjab and British India wars:

Jang Hind Punjab Da Hoan Lagga Dovein Badshahi Faujan Bharian Ni

Ajj Hoveh Sarkar Taan Mull Paweh Jehrian Khalsey Ne Tegha Mrian Ni

......

Shah Muhammada Ik Sarkar Bajon

Faujan Jit ke Ant Noon Harian Ni

> The war between Punjab and India began
>
> Both the royal armies are immense
>
> ......
>
> The Maharaja would have appreciated
>
> The way the Khalsa wielded their swords
>
> ......
>
> Oh Shah Muhammad but for the Maharaja's presence
>
> The armies lost after winning the war

Even after the two wars, the British annexed Lahore in 1849 as a protectorate of the young five year old Prince Daleep Singh. They took him to London and made friends with the Punjab Army and Administration.

Baba Ram Singh (1816-1885) was in Maharaja Ranjit Singh's Army. He left after the first Anglo-Sikh war and **came to settle in a small village, Bheni. He organized a total non-cooperation movement against the British in 1857.** He had participants in every District in Punjab. Later the Indian National congress adopted a similar non-cooperation movement, mentioning that it was inspired by Baba Ram Singh's work. The British encouraged some Muslim butchers to open butcher shops around Sri Durbar Sahib. Sikhs were enraged and saw it as desecration of their shrine. Some of Baba Ram Singh's followers fell into the trap and attacked these butcher shops and a few of the owners were killed. This gave the British an excuse to annihilate the movement of peaceful non-cooperation. They exiled Baba Ram Singh to Andaman Islands and killed sixty-six of his followers with cannonball fire.

Before the British conquered Punjab, the people of that region had a diverse and humanistic administration and lived in peace and prosperity.

IV

The Advent of Colonization
of India by European Powers

Vasco Da Gama from Portugal discovered the sea route to India in 1498. Until that time all the invaders came to India through Khyber Pass, going through Punjab. The Mughals ruled India for almost three hundred years (1526-1857) before the British established Delhi as the Capital of India. For the first time they created a political entity of India as one country. Before them there were only the regional small states run by Nawabs, Maharajas, Nizams and Ranas. The Mughals also contributed substantially to Indian architecture, music, dance, literature and arts. They created Urdu as a national language. The Freedom struggle against them is briefly described above. The discovery of a sea route brought the European powers to colonize India. Emperor Jahangir in 1612 granted the British East India Trading Company the right to have a factory and a trading post in Surat, Gujrat. The Portuguese and the French were their rivals from Europe. By 1857 the British East India Company had major control over the Indian territories. There were small enclaves of French territory in Pondicherry and the Portuguese had Goa.

The British East India Company, through making alliances with Rajas and Nawabs of small states against each other, conquered most of India. There were over 565 Princely States that were under British Protectorate. There were quite a few small-scale rebellions against the British East India Company rule. In 1857 there was a large-scale mutiny against the British. It was inspired by the rumors spread in the British Indian Army that the rifle cartridges had been laced with cow and pig fat. The soldiers had to bite them before loading them into rifles. Muslims do not eat pig and the Hindus hold cows as sacred. There were Princely States that were ready to fight to preserve their rule, such as, Rani of Jhansi. The mutineer persuaded Bahadur Shah-II in Delhi to join them. Thus the mutiny took a national form. The British were quite ill prepared. Once they awakened to the reality of this threat, they were able to squelch this mutiny. There was very little coordination among the mutineers. Then in 1857 the British Government took over the rule of India from the British East India Trading Company and established a British Raj. Queen Victoria added another title to her crown: the Empress of India.

V

Indian National Congress and Freedom Movement against Colonial British Raj

In 1885 under the authority of the British, retired officer Allen Octavian Hume (1829-1912) met with 72 Indian delegates in Bombay to form the Indian National Congress. It was an attempt to have the Indian elite who were educated in the British tradition to represent Indian interests to the government. The Congress members began to have differences and in 1907 there was a split. There were those who were called moderates who wanted to bring about change through constitutional negotiation. They included Dadabai Naoroji and Gopal Krishan Gokhle.

Mr. Muhammad Ali Jinnah joined the Indian National Congress in 1904 and joined this group. The Radical group included Ganga Ram Tilak and lala Lajpat Rai. Tilak said that it was his birthright to have Swaraj (independence) and expressed his want to work toward having it.

Mr. Jinnah was very active in the Indian National Congress for almost two decades. He had a successful law practice. In 1909 he was elected to Imperial Legislative Council. In 1911 he introduced the Wakf Validation Act that allowed Muslim religious trusts to be on firm legal footing. He was also nominated to be a member of the Sand Hurst Committee that helped in creating the Dehra Dun Military Academy. He was a staunch Nationalist and wanted a secular, united India. For example in 1909 a Muslim delegation of 35 persons, headed by the Agha Khan–II, met with Lord Minto. Jinnah at that time questioned who gave them the authority to represent Muslims. He joined the Muslim League in 1913 to bring about reconciliation between Congress and the Muslim League. He continued his membership in the Indian National Congress. Gopal Krishan Gokhle called him an Ambassador of Hindu-Muslim unity. Mr. Jinnah was successful in his mission. In 1916 he was able to pass the Lucknow Pact in both the Muslim League and the Indian National congress. **Unfortunately, it was over turned by Pundit Nehru and Gandhi ji a year later.** Mr. Jinnah resigned from Indian National Congress in 1920 because of his differences with Gandhi ji.

Mr. Jinnah believed that achievement of desirable objectives and change could be accomplished through negotiations and constitutional means, whereas Gandhi ji thought the only way was through passive resistance. In 1920 at the Nagpur Session of the Indian National congress, **Mr. Jinnah was booed off the stage because he addressed Mahatma Gandhi as Mr. Gandhi.**

In 1905 the Viceroy Lord Curzon divided Bengal into East and West Bengal. East Bengal gave Muslims a majority. The Indian National Congress saw it as a divide and rule policy and there was a great opposition. **It was repealed in 1906. The Muslim community felt betrayed. That same year, the Muslim League was formed in Dhaka, East Bengal under the leadership of Sir Syed Ahmed Khan and Vicar-ul-Haq to protect the interests of the Muslim community.** Syed Ahmed Khan also created the Aligarh Muslim University. He believed that the Muslims had to have modern Western education and understanding of their religious roots to advocate for their rights. **He was also a proponent of the Two-Nation theory.** He believed that Muslims could not feel safe under the dominance of a Hindu majority that was totally different from them. They were perceived to have a different culture, religion, with different traditions and diet.

In 1909 a Muslim Delegation of 35 persons representing different provinces of India headed by the Agha Khan-II met with Lord Minto. They were successful in promulgating a Council Act that assured Muslim participation in British Civil Service. In 1928 the British invited input as a preparation for the 1935 Government of India Act that would give India Dominion status. Pundit Nehru recommended that the Legislative Assembly Representatives represent their geographical constituency. This would compel different communities to cooperate and could lead to national integration. This was not accepted. **This was the time to take a stand as a Satyagraha believer. Gandhi ji had confused Satyagraha (meaning to incorporate truth and live by it regardless of the consequences) with his Passive Resistance movement. Accepting elections on the basis of religious affiliation set the stage for the Partition of India. If it was the right thing to do the Indian National Congress should not have yielded. At that time the Indian National congress was still the most dominant political force.** In accordance with the 1935 Government of India Act, provincial Assembly Elections were held in 1937. Each religious group was allocated a number of representatives in proportion to their numbers in residence in each province.

During this election the majority of Muslim representatives belonged to the Indian National congress. Only about 5% of Muslim representatives belonged to the Muslim League. The Congress had a clean sweep and formed a government in eight of the eleven provinces. **The provinces where Congress did not have absolute majority refused to collaborate with the Muslim League to form a Government.**

Nisid Hajari writes in his book Midnight's Furies (2015, page 33) that **Jinnah publically suggested that after the elections, he would be open to throwing the League's Muslim support behind the old comrades in the Congress. Nehru mocked the idea and told reporters in November, 1936:**

> **I thank Mr. Jinnah for the offer but so far as our fight for freedom is concerned, it is going to be carried on by the Congress and the Congress alone.**

Indians of all faiths faced a simple choice in the elections, Nehru declared: either cast their votes for Congress Party or resign themselves to continued servitude to the British.

In 1939 the Congress leadership was quite angry that the Viceroy committed India to join the World War II effort without consulting them. **In Protest the Congress Legislatures resigned from all of the Provincial British India Governments to which they had been elected.** The Muslim League celebrated the end of British India Government led by Indian National Congress.

In 1930 the great poet, intellectual and philosopher Allama Iqbal was elected President of the Muslim League. Originally he was a great patriot. He wrote Tarana-e Hindi (Song of India) in 1904:

> **Saare Jahan Se Achha Hindustan Hamara**
>
> **Hum Bulbulen Hain Is Ki Yeh Gulistan Hamara**
>
> > Our India is the Greatest of All
> >
> > We are its Nightingales and this is our flower garden

Mazahab Nahin Sikhata Appas Mein Ber Rakhna

Hindi Hain Humvatan Hain Hindustan Hamara

Religion does not teach to have enmity with each other

We are Indians and fellow countrymen India belongs to us

He gradually began to advocate Muslim cause as is clear in his

Taranna-e Millat in 1910 where he writes

Cheen-o-Arab Hamara Hindustan Hamara

Muslim Hain Humvatan Hain Sara Jahan Hamara

China, Arab and India belong to us

We are Muslims of the same country
and the whole world belongs to us

During the 1930 session the idea of a separate state for Muslims was introduced. In 1940 during the Muslim League's session in Lahore the resolution was passed demanding a separate state of Pakistan for Muslims.

In 1942 the Indian National Congress launched the Quit India Movement. In response the British Government jailed all the leadership of Congress and placed Gandhi ji on house arrest in one of the Agha Khan's palaces. They were not released until the end of World War II. For reasons that no one has ever explained Mr. Jinnah left India in 1930. Most likely he was dejected by India's political scene. He bought a house in London and began a law practice. He returned to India in 1934, while winding down his practice in London. He returned to London frequently. During the Quit India Movement, the Muslim League did not join and supported the British.

Mr. Jinnah always nurtured his relationship with British Parliamentarians. After one of the failed Round Table Conferences in London, Gandhi ji and Pundit Nehru returned to India. Mr. Jinnah stayed in London for three weeks and met with the British Parliamentarians including Mr. Churchill who opposed transfer of power to the Indians. When he was the Prime Minster he stated that he would not preside over liquidation of the British Empire. He supported Mr. Jinnah hoping to create a wedge to block transfer of power to the Indians. After the Muslim League's support of the war effort during the Quit India Movement, British support for the Muslim League was quite open. In 1940 the British Indian Government pledged to the Muslim League that they would not transfer power to the Indians unless the proposed constitution was first approved by the Muslim League. The promise was never kept but it immensely increased the Muslim League's negotiating power. While all the Congress Leadership was in jail Mr. Jinnah's rallies began to attract audiences larger than in Pundit Nehru or Gandhi ji's rallies. After the war even Jinnah was surprised that he was treated as an equal to Gandhi ji.

Gandhi ji returned to India from South Africa in 1915 at the invitation of Mr. Gopal Krishan Gokhle who also acted as his mentor in introducing him to the Indian political scene. Gandhi ji had considerable success in South Africa fighting against the discriminatory laws and attitudes against the Indians. **He did not want to be treated like the native black people whom he called "savages" and "niggers" in the Africana language.** Later he changed his professed attitude toward the black population to be politically correct.

Gandhi ji became the most senior leader of the Congress after the death of Mr. Gopal Krishan Gokhle and Dadabai Naoroji. Gandhi ji had developed his Passive Resistance strategy against the British he called Satyagraha method as an effective way to fight against such practices. Gandhi ji infused a different life into Congress. He reduced the membership fee to a nominal two Annas; one 8th of a Rupee. He established Pradesh (Provincial) Congress Committees. To appeal to the rural masses Gandhi ji abandoned his Western suits and adopted Indian Dhoti and a big turban. He advocated social reforms, such as, women's equality, a taboo against drinking, the Sati custom, etc. **He changed the Indian National Congress from an elitist group to a people's movement.**

In April 1919 there was a Jallian Wala Bagh massacre in Amritsar, Punjab. During a peaceful gathering for the Harvest Vaisakhi Festival in Jallian Wala Bagh (Park), General Reginald Dyer brought an army battalion and mowed down innocent civilians with machine gun fire. It shook the whole nation. General Dyer was officially reprimanded but was hailed as a hero in London. Sardar Udham Singh followed him to London and shot him to death while Dyer was addressing an audience. There were other revolutionaries inspired by this massacre, such as Bhagat Singh, Raj Guru and Sukhdev. They were Congress members and believed in non-violence until the killing of Lala Lajpat Rai during a peaceful protest.

In the early twenties the Sikhs launched a peaceful protest against the Mahants who occupied historical Gurdwaras including Sri Darbar Sahib (The Golden Temple) in Amritsar and Nankana Sahib, the birthplace of Baba Guru Nanak. The British supported the Mahants. The Mahants were self-imposed guardians of Gurdwaras. They were desecrating the sacred places through very undesirable practices. The Sikhs would go as peaceful Jathas to Nankana Sahib and be mowed down by gunfire and murdered with swords. One of them was burnt alive while strung to a tree. Ultimately the Sikhs prevailed. The British Government passed a Gurdwara Act in 1925 and gave the keys to Sri Darbar Sahib and other historical Gurdwaras to the Shiromani Gurdwara Prabhandhak Committee. The Congress Leadership hailed it as the first victory of the Freedom Struggle of India. The Sikh historical Gurdwaras are still managed by an elected management body called the Shiromani Gurdwara Prabhandhak Committee (SGPC).

In 1919 Gandhi ji launched a non-cooperation movement designed after Baba Ram Singh's non-cooperation movement started in 1857. People were asked to refrain from buying any goods made in England. They were to wear homemade clothes made with cloth from the thread spun from a spinning wheel. He invented a small spinning wheel that was hand-portable. In the Lahore Session in 1929, Congress called for complete independence from British Rule.

Gandhi ji had a very strong reaction to Subhash Chander Bose being elected as the President of Indian National Congress for the second time. He declared that Mr. Bose's election was his own personal defeat. Mr. Bose self-exiled over his differences with Ghandi. During World War II he organized Azad Hind Fauj (the Free India Army) in Japan in collaboration with General Mohan Singh and other British India Army personnel who had deserted the British India Army to join him.

Gandhi ji also came into the limelight during the Salt March that was a success story of the Passive Resistance movement. As a result, Indians could make their salt for personal use from the sea without British interference. On March 5, 1931 the Congress and British signed an

Irwin-Gandhi pact. Gandhi ji represented Indian people through the Indian National Congress and Lord Irwin was the Viceroy of India. The Congress had beseeched Gandhi ji not to sign any pact unless the British released every political prisoner including the three revolutionaries Bhagat Singh, Raj Guru and Sukhdev. Gandhi ji signed the pact without even bringing up the issue. As usual he had a very eloquent defense for what he did.

After World War II the British wanted to transfer power over India to the Indians because they could not afford it financially and because of geopolitical considerations. By this time the Muslim League had emerged as a very powerful force and the sole representation of Muslims. **In the 1946 Provincial Assembly elections, 95% of the Muslim representatives were members of the Muslim League in contrast to only 5% during the 1937 elections. It is obvious that the Indian National Congress had completely alienated the Muslim community.** In summer, 1946, the Hindu-Muslim riots broke out in Noakhli, Bengal, instigated or at least supported by Suhrawardy. He was supported by Gandhi ji during the Khilafat Movement even against the advice of Congress Leadership. Riots in Bihar followed. It was an indiscriminate massacre of Hindus by Muslims and Muslims by Hindus.

After the1946 Provincial elections in Punjab, the Unionist Party formed a collaborative Government under Khizar Hayat Khan Tiwana as Chief Minister.

Mr. Khizar Hayat Khan, knowing the propensity for violence between the Muslim League and Hindu Shiv Sena and Rashtriya Swaym Sevak Sangh (R.S.S.S), banned both parties in Punjab. Unfortunately, I have not found that there was any attempt by Congress leadership to support him. On the other hand, the Muslim League used Gandhian tactics of protest and filled all the jails in Lahore, ultimately forcing Khizar Hayat Khan to resign.

In 1946 Gandhi ji engineered a successful fourth term for Pundit Nehru as President of the Indian National Congress. Lord Wavell, the Viceroy of India, invited Pundit Nehru to form a Government by collaborating with the Muslim League. He asked Nehru to meet with Mr. Jinnah personally. They did meet in Bombay on August 15, 1946. Nisid Jahari writes on page 12 in his book referred to above:

The next morning, before he returned to Delhi, Nehru held (an audience) for reporters. He looked exhausted, as though he hadn't slept.
Still, he affected a cheery insouciance. The lack of agreement between
Congress and the League did not worry him, he insisted, nor did the
possibility that Jinnah's followers might try to topple any Government
led by him. 'In that event,' Nehru said, 'two outcomes were possible.
If the administration showed weakness, the Government would likely
collapse quickly. On the other hand,' he warned, 'if the Government
was strong, the (League's) movement would go down.' To many ears it
sounded like a challenge.

In response to Nehru's comments, **Wavell, in his diary entry for 16
August, "called them as usual – stupid."**

Mr. Jinnah could not stomach the idea of serving as the younger man's
deputy, nor would he allow Congress to include any Muslims in their
own quota of Ministers. In his press release he stated archly, "I know
nothing as to what has transpired between Viceroy and you." If Nehru
was suggesting that he serve in a Congress dominated government,
though, it was obviously "not possible for me to accept such a position."

It seemed that Congress had already decided to accept defeat with partition and betray the aspirations of freedom fighters. Maulana Azad in
his book India Wins Freedom described the Indian National Congress
Working Committee meeting. Maulana ji did not expect much from Sardar Patel. He was disappointed to find out that even Pundit Nehru was
going to support the resolution to accept partition. Maulana ji went to
Gandhi ji and Gandhi ji also answered him that it was a political reality
that they had to accept. You would not expect such a reply from someone who practiced Satya Graha and said repeatedly that India would be
divided over his dead body. Satya Graha means to incorporate Truth
and live by it regardless of consequences. We have examples of Satya
Grahis in human history, such as, Moses, Christ, Muhammad, Baba
Guru Nanak-Guru Gobind Singh. In spite of Gandhi ji, Pundit Nehru
and Sardar Patel's betrayal, the resolution passed with a vote of 29 to 15
in favor of partition of India. Maulana ji did not mention the names of
the individuals who voted against the resolution in his book, the true
Satyagrahis. **They should be celebrated, not the failed politicians who
betrayed India.**

What followed the acceptance of the Partition of India was a humanitarian disaster unparalleled in history. There was massive genocide on both sides of the border in Punjab alone. It is estimated that a million people were killed and there was a forced migration of eighteen million people. Similar events occurred in Bengal. **All of this was inspired by India's political leadership. It was not the result of hatred between Hindu and Muslim Communities. The neighbors and friends on both sides of the border tried to protect their neighbors and friends from the politically inspired violent mobs who were also motivated by their own personal greed and impulses to banditry and rape of women.**

VI

The Populace Experience

Most of what I have read in the literature on the struggle for the Freedom of India is written to reflect the political parties involved and their leadership. **As it becomes more evident that the political leadership and ruling class do not necessarily represent the people,** the Indian leadership did not either. I want to briefly present my perceptions as a person on the street. Until 1946 we lived in Amritsar at Sardar Bahadur Hukam Singh Estate. I attended Sant Singh Sukha Singh Khalsa Middle School. During this time three of the officers of Azad Hind Fauj were jailed in the Red Fort in Delhi. They were accused of treason because they had deserted the British India Army to organize Azad Hind Fauj, the army to fight for India's independence. A trial took place in November-December, 1945 and they were released in January, 1946. I remember all of the students from our school marching on the Mall Road and protesting for the release of these officers. They chanted:

Lal Qileh Se Ayee Awaz

Sehgal Dhillon Shahnawaz

A voice came from Red Fort

Sehgal, Dhillon, Shah Nawaz

Of the three officers, Sehgal was a Hindu, Dhillon was a Sikh and Shahnawaz was a Muslim. There were similar demonstrations all over India. At the populace level there was fervor of communal harmony. At the same time there was a palpable tension and anxiety about what may be happening at the leadership level. There were incidences of stabbing around Rambagh garden.

There were numerous Indian organizations that were fighting for freedom for united India. The Indian diaspora on the Pacific Coast of the United States and Canada organized a Gadar (Mutiny) Party at the turn of the twentieth Century. Founded in 1913, it dissolved in 1919. The Stockton Gurdwara in California was their meeting place. They moved their headquarters to 5 Wood Street in San Francisco and commenced printing of literature in Punjabi, Urdu and Gujrati languages. They had connections with almost all of the revolutionary parties around the world who were fighting for independence from British Colonial rule. In 1960 I met the last Secretary of the Gadar Party, Sardar Jagat Singh. He gave me a picture of himself presenting a sword of honor at Saint Francis Hotel to Emanon De Valera, the Irish revolutionary who later became the President of Ireland. They felt betrayed by the Indian National Congress for accepting the partition of India. The Gadar Party represented the Indian community on the West Coast of Canada and the United States. There were Sikhs, Muslims and Hindus. At that time Punjabis comprised the majority of the immigrants. Gujratis were the second most in numbers.

In 1963 when I began living in the San Francisco Bay Area, I met Mr. Dhillon and Mr. Patel who had organized a Gadar Memorial Committee to establish a memorial in the memory of the persons who had organized this freedom party and died for freedom. The Indian Parliament had allocated $80,000 to build a memorial at 5 Wood Street, the headquarters of the Gadar Party. It was not until Sardar Swaran Singh was the Foreign Minister and Mr. Arora came to San Francisco as Counsel General that a Gadar Memorial Hall was built. (It is unfortunate that in several areas, only Sikh organizations celebrate their memory, making it look like a Sikh sectarian struggle.) The Sikhs are usually in the forefront fighting for the oppressed and maltreated. Gadar Party represented all Indian communities fighting for freedom for a united India. Babbar Akalis and the Kuka Sikh movements were active in Punjab since 1857.

There were also many divisive forces. The Hindu Mahasabha, Rashtrya Swayam Sevak Sangh (RSS) and Shiv Sena were the Hindu communal organizations. The current Prime Minister, Mr. Narinder Modi, has these organizations as his political base. The Muslim League was fighting to protect Muslim interests. On the other hand, the Indian National Congress had totally alienated the Muslim Community because of Gandh ji and Pundit Nehru's egotistical dominance, giving Congress a cult like nature. The Akali Party that represented Sikhs joined the Indian National Congress. The Hindu communal elements never joined the congress. They treated Muslims as "foreigners" who did not belong in India. RSS had branches in almost every city. They would go into neighborhoods to recruit Hindu and Sikh children and youth to join their Shakhas (branches).

At Amritsar these Shakha Leaders came to our neighborhood and wanted us to join their group. I asked them what they do there. They said they just get together to play. I invited all my friends to go. When we arrived, the Shakha leader took me aside and told me that two of my friends did not belong there. I asked him why. He told me that they are Muslims, foreigners and do not belong in India. We never went back to the Shakha. It did not mean that they gave up on us. They came back again and again to convince me that Muslims were our enemies by misrepresenting Sikh history. They gave me examples of Mughal atrocities and cruel murders of the sons of Guru Gobind Sing ji. I reminded them that the Sikh Guru's struggle was against tyrannical rule and that although the emperor happened to be Muslim, the struggle had the populace support of Muslims and Hindus alike.

Baba Guru Nanak had as his lifelong companion the Muslim Rabab player, Mardana. The first person recognized Baba Guru Nanak as a spiritual guide was the Muslim Chief Rai Bular. He transferred half of his estate to Baba Guru Nanak before he died (by personal account of his decedents to the author). This is where all the Gurdwaras in Nankana Sahib were built. During the first battle between the Hindu Pahari Rajas who supported Emperor Aurangzeb it was Pir Budhu Shah, a Muslim Sufi Saint with six hundred of his followers, who fought on the side of Sri Guru Gobind Singh ji. Pir Budhu Shah lost two of his sons along with many of his followers. All through the history of Khalsa fighting against the tyrannical Mughal Empire, Hindus and Muslims alike supported the Khalsa warriors. The Hindu, Diwan Todar Mal, collected all his wealth and sold all his wife's jewelry to arrange the funeral of Guru Gobind Singh's younger two sons and mother. Suba Sirhand wanted to have a spread of 7,800 gold coins equal to the land needed for cremation. Later on Diwan's family lost their lives because of their support of Sri Guru Gobind Singh ji.

In 1946 my father Sardar Puran Singh retired from Punjab Agriculture Service and built a modest house in Rupar, rather than return to our nearby village, Kheri Salabat Pur. I was selected to represent India in the World Scout Jamboree in Paris. My late brother Professor T.S. Saini, Ph.D. invited me to Lahore, where he was working at that time, to learn Western etiquette. This was the spring of 1947. There were already bomb blasts in certain parts of Lahore. The rumors of riots were rampant. In the evenings we played badminton at the Y.M.C.A. and had dinner at Western style hotels such as Falleti's. I spent a month there before I returned to Rupar. This is where I was during the Partition in August, 1947. Unfortunately, I could not attend the Jamboree because of massacres during the partition. My late brother Professor H.S. Dilgir was studying for his Masters in Journalism in Delhi. He wrote me a several-paged letter, enclosing my picture, published in the Liberator, to console me. He quoted a couplet from Allama Iqbal's poem Trana-e Hind:

Mazhab Nahin Sikhata Apas mein Ber Rakhna

Hindi Hain Hum Watan Hain Hindustan Hamara

Religion does not teach us to have enmity with each other

We are Indians and fellow countrymen and India belongs to us

My late brother Dilgir made the following change

Insan Hain Hum Watan Hain Sara Jahan Hamara

We are humans and fellow global citizens
the whole world belongs to us

We lived in the outskirts of town off Hospital Road near the morgue. The first casualty that my sister Bhag and I saw was a very gentle person. I remember his name was Ghani. He drove a Tonga for a living. He was brought to the morgue in his own Tonga. I do not know why our eyes filled with tears. We only knew him because at times he would bring our guests from the train station or bus stop. He was a very kind person.

When the riots broke out we would take turns watching for any mobs coming near us from the roof of our house with my father's double barrel gun. We would hear rifle fire periodically. A retired army officer lived in our neighborhood. He organized a group of men to attack Sheikhan Da Mohalla, a very well to do Muslim neighborhood. The men would return home with trunks full of loot from their attacks on the Muslim neighborhoods. The government evacuated the Muslims to refugee camps in the hills across the Sirhand Canal.

A couple of months later I received a post card from my high school Urdu teacher, Maulvi Nazir-ud-Din Jaffrey, that he had reached Jhang Manghiana in Pakistan after sacrificing his two sons and his wife. He wrote to me that God had given me a gift of public speaking and if I ever spoke I should remember the following two couplets:

Havas Ne Kar Dia Hai Tukre Tukre Nau-e-Insan Ko

Akhwat Ka Bian Ho Ja Muhabat Ki Zaban Ho Ja

Lust has torn humanity into bits and pieces

Be a spokesperson for humanity and a voice of love

Alama Iqbal

Sadma Aa Jai Gul Ki Patti Ko Agar

Ashk Ban Kar Meri Ankhon Se Beh Jai Asar

If a flower's petal is hurt

The impact should flow through the tears from my eyes

Meer Asar

Our S.K. Khalsa High School was turned into a refugee camp. I spent about a year working in that camp. If I remember correctly most of the refugees came from Bahawalpur. Having lost everything including the lives of some of their family members their resilience to deal with the situation left an indelible mark on me.

Political leaders on both sides of the border celebrated their "achievements" with fireworks. Pundit Nehru made his infamous speech

about the Tryst With Destiny. Meanwhile the voices of the populace on both sides of the border in Punjab were full of lamentations, best expressed by the following two poets:

Faiz Ahmed Faiz, from his poem Subah-e-Aazadi

Yeh Daagh Daagh Ujaala Yeh Shab Guzeda Sehar

Woh Intzar Tha Jis Ka Yeh Woh Sehar To Nahin

This spotted dawn and the morning engulfed in darkness of night

This dawn is not the dawn we were waiting for

Faiz Ahmad Faiz from **Lahore** suddenly became a Pakistani Urdu Poet.

Amrita Pritam from **Lahore** became a refugee Indian Punjabi poet. She wrote her poem Ajj Akhaan Waris Shah Nu

Ajj Akhan Waris Shah Nu Kiton Kabran Vichon Bol

Te Ajj Kitab-e-Ishk Da Koi Agla Varka Phol

Ik Roee See Dhee Punjab Di Toon Likh Likh Maarey Vain

Ajj Lakhan Dhian Rondian, Tainu Waris Shah Nu Kehn

Veh Dard Mandan Dea Dardia, Tak Aa Ke Punjab

Ajj Bele Lashaan Vichhian Te Lahoo Di Bhari Chanab.

Amrita Pritam

Today I want to ask Waris Shah to speak from his grave

Today explore the next page of love

One daughter of the Punjab cried

You wrote thousands upon thousands of lamentations

Today millions of daughters are crying out for Waris Shah

Oh the one who shared others pain

Was the voice of people's pain

Come and look at your Punjab

The meadows that were the lover's tryst

Are littered with dead bodies

The romantic river of Chanab

Is all filled with blood

The genocide on both sides of the border was committed by the politically inspired mobs. **The political leadership of India and the British Administration were directly responsible for it.** On both sides of the border people tried to save their neighbors and friends from this mob violence. I will share one such example. My friend Gurbax Singh Thind's uncle, Dr. Khushdev Singh of Patiala, wrote a short book describing this incident. When a mob came to attack the Muslim villages the Sikhs from neighboring villages created a human chain and told the mob members that they had to kill them first before they could harm their neighbors. They saved about 10,000 lives. In 1974 I visited Pakistan with my friend Mr. Vajid Jafri, I saw one of the survivors of that incident. At that time, he was the Minister of Rehabilitation in Pakistan. Dr. Khushdev Singh had given me a copy of his book to deliver to his friend in Pakistan. I sent in my visiting card a note that I was Dr. Khushdev Singh's nephew. The Minister came out to greet me. He gave me such a loving embrace with teary eyes the loving memory of which even now brings tears to my eyes!

When Gandhi ji was assassinated in January 1948, the Sikhs and Muslims were very frightened. If the assassin were a Sikh or Muslim, there would be Hindu mob attacks. Soon it was in the news that a Hindu gentleman, Nathu Ram Godsey, had shot Gandhi ji. The Indian National Congress was immensely despised. When I went to Patiala to attend Mahendra College in 1948 they erected Gandhi ji's statue in King Edward's Tank. On the next day they found a garland of broken shoes around his neck. This is a symbol of great humiliation. The next day someone chopped off the head of the statue. They had to have a twenty-four hour guard to protect the statue.

Almost 65 years after the partition a young woman, Dr. Guneeta Singh Bhalla, has created an organization, The 1947 Partition Archives. Interviews from all over the world have been videotaped with persons who had experienced the partition events. It is a rare record of the suffering of people. **One expression in common among the interviewees is nostalgia for life in pre-partition times.** They miss their ancestral homes, their neighbors and friends. Surprisingly, instead of bitterness they pray for peace in the world.

When Pakistani Punjabis visit Indian Punjab as tourists or to attend sports or cultural events, the Indian Punjabis greet them as long lost family. The same is true when Indian Punjabis visit Pakistan. A few years ago I was in Lahore. I asked the hotel front desk to send someone to get my internet connection going. A young man in his early twenties came and helped me with my internet connection. While leaving he turned around said with teary eyes that his family came from a village near Hoshiarpur. His father wanted to take his family to India and show them their ancestral home and meet the people there. He never could get a visa and died without having the opportunity to show his ancestral village to his family. When the Sikh pilgrims go to Pakistan on Nankana Sahib pilgrimage, the young man goes to meet them to see if any one of them is from his ancestral village.

I have never received as much love anywhere else as I received from the people of Pakistan. The shopkeepers and the persons on the street would greet me with love. During my last visit my friend had gone into a store and I stayed in the car. A fakir approached the car singing Baba Guru Nanak's Shabad from the sacred book Sri Guru Granth Sahib (SGGS 954).

Nanak Dukhia Sabh Sansar

Oh Nanak everyone is suffering in this world.

VII

The Leaders at the time of the Transfer of Power

It is the moon that has room for spots not the stars.

Tagore

The very fact that I am spending so much time and effort to review their contribution toward India and Pakistan's freedom struggle speaks to the fact that these were no ordinary men. Numerous others have written about them and there will be more to come. **My main purpose is to fig-**

ure out what we can learn from this experience, to liberate ourselves from a paradigm that does not get us anywhere or, worse, continues to lead us toward our own destruction.

It is obvious from the brief description of India's struggle above that five persons dominated the course of history at that time. There were many other persons and movements that contributed to or detracted from the struggle. But at the time of the transfer of power from the British, the standouts were the Lord Mountbatten (Viceroy of India), Gandhi ji, Pundit Nehru, Qaid-e-Azam Muhammad Ali Jinnah, Maulana Abu-ul Kalam Azad and Sardar Vallabhai Patel. I will share my understanding of each of these personalities and how they impacted the struggle.

Gandhi ji: He was a very charismatic leader. He transformed the Indian National Congress from an elitist organization to a populist movement by establishing provincial leadership and enabled ordinary persons to join the party with a minimal membership fee. He changed his dress from Western suits to an Indian peasant look. **He led a non-cooperation movement featuring peaceful protest, public relations and marketing strategies. A also was a great writer, though there were a lot of contradictions between what he wrote about and what he did.**

He wanted to identify with ordinary people therefore he would travel by train in third class compartments. The only difference was that he did not travel like any other Indian jostling to get in to a very packed compartment. As a boy I saw his pictures in the Tribune. His lady devotees escorted him and fanned him. His followers occupied the whole compartment. No ordinary other person was in the compartment. It was a great show. Contrast it with Pope Francis. As a Bishop in Argentina he travelled by public transportation and served the poor and neglected. There were hardly any special arrangements or publicity.

Gandhi ji claimed to champion the cause of oppressed Shudras (untouchables). He called them Harijans (Children of Krishna) **that was quite patronizing. In 1936 he blocked the presentation of Dr. Ambedkar's article, advocating the rights of these oppressed people. It is only recently that the same writings of Dr. Ambedkar were published by Arundatti Roy. Gandhi ji employed his usual power tactics and went on a hunger strike to prevent the separate representation of these oppressed people. He wanted them to be counted as Hindus. His sense of personal superiority is a common thread in his own life. Even in Africa he did** not protest against the oppression of people. He protested that Indians should not be lumped together with the black native "savages."

I do not know who gave Mahatma ji this title. It means that he was a great soul or a saint. For hundreds of years before him spiritual beings from all parts of India had debunked ritualistic practices. They emphasized love for the Creator and Its Creation, living a householder's life, earning an honest living and sharing with the needy. He vowed celibacy when he was 35 years old. In 1946, feeling quite defeated politically, he started sleeping naked with his teenage grandniece to test his strength of celibacy and regain his inner spiritual powers. He championed the equality of women yet was abusive to his own wife. He continuing sleeeping naked with other naked women to test his powers of celibacy.

Gandhi ji wanted to create Ram Rajya based on the hero of the Hindu epic, Ramayana King Rama. I do not find any systematic description of such a rule. On the other hand, there was an outstanding example of a humanistic and completely integrated rule in Northwest India, in a territory that is now mostly part of Pakistan, where everyone lived in peace just before the British India Army invaded Punjab in 1849. As mentioned before, Maharaja Ranjit Singh was a Sikh, his Foreign Minister and Chief Counsel was the Muslim Sufi Saint Fakir Aziz-ud-Din and his Prime Minister was the Hindu Dogra Dhayan Singh. The Khalsa army of Punjab was over 50% non-Sikhs. It had Muslims, Sikhs, Hindus and European generals. Gandhi ji never studied about how such an achievement happened (that the native sons of India for the first time had created an ideal regime). Historians agree that for 50 years of this regime in Punjab, Hindus, Sikhs, Muslims and Christians lived in complete harmony.

After the death of Gopal Krishan Gokhle and Dadabai Naoroji, Gandhi ji became the most senior leader. Pundit Nehru became his protégé. There was no tolerance for views that were not approved by Gandhi ji. We lost the voices of Subhash Chandar Bose and Dr. Ambedkar. We lost one of the most capable of Indian National Congress leaders in Mr. Jinnah to the Muslim League because he had a different point of view than Gandhi ji. His views were not incompatible with non-violence protests when necessary but Mr. Jinnah wanted to follow the constitutional means. He proved his mettle by getting what the Muslim League wanted, using his superior power of strategic thinking.

Gandhi ji's passive resistance tactics are his major claim to fame. He and other writers use passive resistance and Satyagraha inter-changeably. Satyagraha means to incorporate truth and live by it regardless of the consequence. Truth stands for eternal truth; Divine love. Moses could be Satayagrahi because he loved the oppressed slaves, gave up his most powerful position and lived through the consequences, even at the peril of his life. Similarly, Christ, Hazarat Muhammad, Baba Guru Nanak, Guru Arjan Dev, Guru Tegh Bahadur, Guru Gobind Singh and many other such persons practiced Satyagraha. **The basis of Gandhi ji's passive resistance was motivated by anger not love.** At times he succeeded by his stubbornness. Just think of a family system. At times a stubborn child gets his way with the parents. Siblings may react to this. Usually such a stubborn child is resented by his siblings. Gandhi ji never tried to collaborate or compromise with peer leaders who did not totally follow him. He had no awareness or skills in negotiating or compromising with his peers. Gandhi ji wrote that his major regret in life was his inability to **persuade** Mr. Jinnah or his son.

If you notice in Gandhi ji's statement his main objective was to **persuade** others to accept his position, not to understand the other person's point of view with love and come up with some kind of mutual understanding. At the time of Nelson Mandela's death, the former Prime Minister of India, Dr. Manmohan Singh, said while conveying his condolences that Nelson Mandela was a true Gandhian. I do not know if that is a true compliment. Gandhi ji either got rid of persons who he did not agree with him, like Subhash Chander Bose and Dr. Ambedkar, or made adversaries like Mr. Jinnah and his son. Gandhi ji presided over the division and destruction of his country by alienating others. On the other hand, **Nelson Mandela tried to learn Africana while he was in jail and tried to understand his opponents. When he had a chance he established a Truth Commission to bring adversaries together who had been involved in killing each other.**

Gandhi ji had no awareness of how much his thinking was dominated by the Hindu mindset. His vocabulary did not express common Indian language. He called the opporessed scheduled castes as Harijans - a Hindu metaphor. He wanted them to be counted as Hindus. He was a Ram Rajaya and not use a concept representing Indian expression. He insisted Dalits be considered as Hindus for the Hindu vote bank. Jinnah and other non-Hindus could see his façade as a national leader. Non-

Hindu leaders could see through it. Mr. Jinnah, at the death of Ghandi ji, mentioned in his condolence message that Ghandi-ji was a great Hindu leader. The Hindu parties resented him because they thought he was going out of his way to appease the Muslim community. He did not show any skills or interest in developing understanding and bringing people together. He thought his power tactics like passive resistance or fasting unto death were the panacea for every situation. Unfortunately the Indian National Congress Party ruled India for decades after India's partition. It promoted a one-sided, false narrative of India's Freedom Movement and supported the production of a Gandhi movie that is a fictionalized account of the man.

Pundit Jawaharlal Nehru: Pundit Nehru was a true believer in secular government. He was more transparent about what he stood for. He followed Gandhi ji unconditionally except near the end when Gandhi ji offered Mr. Jinnah to be the Prime Minister and lead the Indian government administration. At that point Pundit Nehru and Sardar Patel gently opposed him. Nehru was more humble in his assessment of India's Freedom achievement. In the sixties he commented that at the time of transfer of power they were tired and getting old. He did not try to justify their decision. He had developed an intense personal dislike for Mr. Jinnah and the Muslim League. He called the Muslim League evil and compared it to the Nazi party. How would you expect cooperation from someone you despise so much?

He had the right idea in 1935 when he stated that the Provincial Assembly representatives should be elected according to geographical constituencies and not because of religious affiliations. Unfortunately they did not fight for it. The Indian National Congress leadership during the Gandhi-Nehru era consistently made mistakes to alienate Mr. Jinnah and the Muslim League. They went back on the Lucknow Pact that protected the rights of the Muslim minority. They refused to collaborate with the Muslim League in the three provinces where congress did not have an absolute majority. If Congress was totally non-cooperative with Muslim League, how did they expect that Muslim League should collaborate with them?

Mr. Jinnah offered that the Muslim League could work with Congress and Pundit Nehru scoffed at it. Somehow, at some point, Gandhi-Nehru forgot that they were responsible for all Indians, not just to promote the

Indian National Congress Party. In 1947 the Indian National Congress did not support Khizar Hayat Khan Tiwana in Punjab where he was facing the Muslim League and Shiv Sena alike. One could conjecture that since Pundit Nehru was so vehement about the Indian National Congress being the only custodian of negotiations for India's freedom, this precluded interest in supporting another secular Unionist party.

Maulan Azad mentions in his book India Wins Freedom that Pundit Nehru was very perturbed during the transfer of power. His sleep was very disturbed and he would mutter in his sleep. It was very hard on them to have failed in their struggle for freedom. One can be compassionate and more importantly learn from this tragic experience. Nevertheless, it is not useful to glorify their failure. I quote a paragraph from Nisid Hijari's book Midnight Furies (page 158):

> **One night a Muslim friend named Badurddin Tayabji showed up at Nehru's door to alert him to an especially troubled area – the Minto Bridge, which Muslims fleeing their old Delhi neighborhoods had to cross to reach the safety of refugee camps in New Delhi. Each night, Tayabji said, gangs of Sikhs and Hindus lurked nearby and sprung on the defenseless Muslims as they trudged pass. Nehru immediately bolted from his seat and dashed upstairs. He returned a few minutes later holding a dusty, ungainly revolver. The gun had once belonged to his father Motilal, and hadn't been fired for years. He had a plan, he told Tayabji. They will don soiled clothes and torn Kurtas and drive up to Minto Bridge themselves that night. Disguised as refugees, they would come cross the bridge, and when the thugs tried to way lay them, 'we would shoot them down!' The stunned Tayabji was able to persuade the leader of the world's second biggest Nation only with a great difficulty that 'some less hazardous and more effective method could be devised.' Mountbatten feared Nehru's impulsiveness would get him killed, and assigned soldiers watch over him.**

The above quote could have come from a very entertaining, hilarious comedy skit if only it was not tragically true about the failed leadership of the Indian National Congress. Mr. Nehru had shown similar behavior repeatedly in other instances. The Gandhians practiced a very strange and egotistical stubborn kind of non-violence. They practiced non-violence when facing a powerful enemy. When they had to deal with persons who were not as powerful they could abuse them and humiliate them and be quite violent toward them. There were many more effective means at their disposal. If Pundit ji wanted to use his influence he could have gone to the so-called Hindu and Sikh thugs and expressed compassion that he understood that many of them were themselves refugees and suffered losses. These refugees had nothing to do with their losses. They themselves were the victims. There were many other persons who had diffused violent mobs by talking to them. They had nowhere near the influence of Pundit Nehru.

Qaid-e-Azam Muhammad Ali Jinnah: Mr. Jinnah was a nationalist leader. Gandhi ji marginalized him and promoted Pundit Nehru because Nehru became his disciple even though he was much more junior to Jinnah and had very little to show for himself except he was Motilal Nehru's son. Previously Mr. Jinnah had the respect of Congress leaders because of his ability and contributions and devotion to the nationalist cause. After the death of Ram Krishan Gokhle, Gandhi ji became the most senior leader and did not respect ideas other than his own. Mr. Jinnah tried several times and he was rebuffed.

Mr. Jinnah became quite suspicious of Gandhi ji and Nehru's assertions. He began to see them espousing the Hindu majority cause and not representing or protecting minority rights.

Gandhi ji was equally intolerant of other leaders who did not unconditionally follow him, such as Subhash Chander Bose and Dr. Ambedkar. Unfortunately, Mr. Jinnah took it personally and saw it as the disregard of the Muslim minority. Even though Pakistan is named Islamic Republic of Pakistan, Mr. Jinnah protected the rights of minorities in Pakistan's constitution.

Sardar Vallabhbai Patel: He was quite an independent and strong-minded leader. He was very disenchanted with Pundit Nehru and Gandhi ji's inability to negotiate and make compromise. **He saw them as either protesting or placating.** At the time of transfer of power, without consulting Pundit Nehru and Gandhi ji, he collaborated with Lord Mountbatten and persuaded around 550 rulers of the Princely States to join India. Nizams of Hydrabad and Junagarh were negotiating with Jinnah to join Pakistan but Patel and Mountbatten had them join India by force. Pundit Nehru had a special interest in Kashmir, maybe because his ancestors came from there. He wanted to deal with Kashmir himself and made a mess of the situation over which India and Pakistan are still fighting.

Pakistan created and supported an army of Tribal People from Pakistan to declare Jihad against India and invade Kashmir, the rationale being to free Kashmir because the majority of the population was Muslim. The Hindu Maharaja of Kashmir and the Muslim Prime Minister of Kashmir, Sheikh Abdullah, flew to Delhi and signed the accession treaty to join India. At the time of partition, the Princely States had the option to join India, Pakistan or remain independent. Kashmir decided to remain independent. After Pakistan and its surrogate Tribal People had invaded Kashmir the Indian Government (post-treaty) sent the Indian army to fight the invaders. The Indian army started pushing the invading army out of Kashmir. The Prime Minister of India, Pundit Nehru, took the matter to the Security Council and a ceasefire was declared at the current line of control. There was supposed to be a plebiscite for the Kashmiri people to decide whether they wanted to stay independent or join India or Pakistan. Neither India nor Pakistan fulfilled the preconditions for the plebiscite and the issue remains unresolved. Pakistani militants continued the murder of Hindus in Kashmir. There are three hundred thousand Hindu refugees from Kashmir. A couple of years ago Muslim militants went to a Sikh village in Kashmir and massacred over 60 men of the village. **There have been three wars between India and Pakistan. This conflict is the continuation of the narrative of the absurd Two Nation theory. India, Pakistan and Kashmir are still enslaved by Two Nation theory, doing the bidding of powers that follow a policy of divide and rule. Where is the Independence from divisive politics? What kind of independence do Indian and Pakistani leadership celebrate every year!**

Maulana Abu-ul-Kalam Azad: He was a great scholar of Islamic Religion and Indian history. He was in the forefront of India's struggle for freedom. Fortunately he was not educated in the West. He stuck to Indian values. In the book India Wins Freedom he described the debate in the Indian National Congress Working Committee in June, 1947 whether or not India should accept partition of India. He was appalled by the nature of speeches that were made. Some speakers claimed that if the Hindus were mistreated in Pakistan, they would take it out on the Muslims in India in retaliation. No Congress leader can pretend that they had no indication or part to play in the human catastrophe that

followed the Partition. At the end of 1947 debate 29 persons supported
the partition including Gandhi ji, Pundit Nehru and Sardar Patel. In
spite of the prestige of Gandhi, Nehru and Sardar Patel, fifteen persons
voted against partition including Maulana Azad. These people should
be celebrated rather than the leaders who betrayed the aspirations of the
Freedom fighters.

Lord Mountbatten: He was given an impossible task. For economic
and geopolitical reasons the British government was in a hurry to leave
India. He was to transfer power within a few months. In Lord Mountbatten, England had sent one of their most able leaders to complete this
task. There is no question that the transition of power to the Indians and
Pakistanis should have been better thought through and properly ex-
ecuted. The unprecedented human tragedy could have been prevented.
Nevertheless Lord Mountbatten did his best. He was charming and had
the ability to keep a positive working relationship with both Indian and
Pakistani leadership. He did one good thing for India. He and Sardar
Patel are responsible for integrating over 550 Princely States into India.

VIII

The Answer

Baal-O-Pur Tor Kar Syad Kare Hai Azad

Yeh Azadi Hai Kis Kaam Ki!

    The captor gives freedom

    After tearing apart my hair and wings

    What use is this freedom?

By now you must have guessed my answer to the question, did India and
Pakistan win freedom? The Indians were able to get their captors out
of the country. In the process they lost their soul and the ability to live
in peace and prosperity. It took over six centuries to create a spiritual
unity among the people of India. It was blown to smithereens by the
partitioning of the country on the basis of religion. The people of the
subcontinent have not yet recovered from it. The region is totally desta-
bilized. India and Pakistan have had three wars. They have wasted their

resources on military budgets instead of providing economic prosperity, heath, education and welfare services to their people. The colonists have not changed their tactics of divide and rule. Now it is divide and profit. They maintain their dominance and exploit the resources of countries around the world. India's resources are being drained out by numerous multinational corporations in contrast with just one East India Trading Company's doing so during colonization of India. The political leaders have not changed their ways nor learned any lessons. I will enumerate a few lessons to be learned below.

Us Ko Falak Ne Loot Key Vairan Kar Diya

Hum Rahne Wale Hain Ussi Ujre Diyar Ke

That place that was robbed and devastated by the skies

We are the inhabitants of that desolate place

IX

Learning and its Current Geopolitical Implications

The tragedy of India is repeated again and again and we have been unable to change course away from our destruction. Today, there are tens of millions of refugees worldwide who are escaping the ravages of war created by our insatiable lust for dominance and greed. We could blame inept leadership that is motivated by greed for their self promotion and use of patriotism, religion or other emotional symbols to dominate others and exploit the resources of other countries in their own misconceived self-interest and for their corporate friends. **However, in reality, we get the kind of leadership that we collectively create and deserve.**

1. Political Policy of Divide and Profit: It was successfully used in India to destroy by dividing the country on the basis of religion. India and Pakistan are still following the same narrative. They have had three wars. They have used their resources to build atomic weapons and military strength instead of providing health, education and human welfare services for their people. The United States used the same strategy in invading Iraq to destroy a secular regime and create conflict between Sunnis and Shias. The motive was to exploit the oil resources of Iraq. If you follow the money, the invasion provided no help for the people of the

United States. It did financially rescue the Halle-Burton Corporation, whose former C.E.O. Dick Chaney became Vice President of the United States. Because of the money spent on war and the war machine there is no money left for health, education and welfare. This policy continues all over the world and is for the benefit of the few.

For further details please see selected bibliography III Political Economics Page 107 and V. Interventions and Regime Change Page 108.

George Washington warned us in his farewell address that war is one of the major factors that will destroy Democracy. He also warned against over-identification with party politics instead of keeping the focus on what is good for the country. Now we live in a "Global Village" and the focus should be on what is good for the global population. Similarly, we need to refrain from over-promotion of party and other sectarian or patriotic agenda that are not in the interest of the people on this planet. We are here to live in peace and prosperity together or perish together. The stakes are too high now that we have the capacity to destroy all life on this planet. Or we could make this planet a living heaven for all of us!

A hopeful sign is that the people of most countries have awakened to the fact that their governments are not functioning in their best interest. There was the Egyptian Spring revolution that toppled the Dictator Hosni Mubarak. Unfortunately, he was quickly replaced by a worse dictator that the United States continue to support. In the United States there was the Occupy Wall Street movement that was brutally destroyed. In India the Aam Adami (Common Man) party won the Delhi legislative elections by a landslide but it could not govern competently and was marred by corruption. The point is that as people are awakened; it will only be a matter of time before they will free themselves of self-centered and corrupt leadership in their own country. As before when people became aware of the foreign rules it was only a matter of time before they got rid of those rulers. Change has to begin within our educational system to emphasize humanistic values instead of greed, lust for power, dominance and exploitation of natural resources for the benefit of the few

For further details see Selected Bibliography VII. Awakening and Hope. Page 111.

2. Freedom from Oneself: We get the leader we deserve. They represent us. If we want to change from the course of destruction and have better leaders we need to start with the education of children in each of our countries. The wars and atrocities are created by persons who have graduated from the top universities of their countries, such as Harvard, Yale, Oxford and Cambridge etc. These universities do not teach their students **freedom from themselves,** that is, from misguided pursuits of power, greed and exploitation of others for misconceived vested interest.

For more detailed information see Selected Bibliography I. Freedom From Oneself Page 105.

We need to teach from the beginning of education the skills to resolve conflicts peacefully at the intra-psychic, inter-personal, organizational, national and international levels. Teach children how destructive consumerism is? We think we consume goods to satisfy our greed and pursuit of power. Rather, they consume us and destroy human relationships. We have to cure ourselves of egocentric addictions in order to have some hope for humanity. The following quote of Steve Jobs, the creator of Apple Computers, just before he died, may be of useful guidance for the coming generations:

> **I have come to the pinnacle of success of business in the eyes of others; my life is a symbol of success. However, apart from work, (I) have little joy; finally my wealth is simply a fact to which I am accustomed. At this time, lying on the hospital bed and remembering my life I realize that all the accolades and riches of which I was proud, have become insignificant, with my imminent death. In the dark, when I look at green lights, of the equipment for artificial respiration and feel the buzz of their mechanical sounds, I can feel the breath of my approaching death looming over me. Only now do I understand that once you accumulate enough money for the rest of your life, you have to pursue objectives that are not related to wealth. It should be something more important, for example, stories of love, art, dreams of my childhood. No, stop pursuing wealth. It can only make a person into a twisted being, just like me. God has made us one way, we can feel the love in the heart of each of us, not illusions built on fame or money, like I made in my life, I cannot take it with me. I can only take with me the memories that were strengthened by love. This is the true wealth that will follow you, will give you strength and light to go ahead. Love can travel thousands of miles and so life has no limits. Move to where**

you want to go, strive to reach the goals you want to achieve. Everything is in your heart and in your hands. What is the most expensive bed? The hospital bed. If you have money, you can hire someone to drive your car. You cannot hire someone to take your illness that is killing you. Material things lost can be found. But you can never find once you (have) lost it, life. Whatever stage of life where you are now, at the end we have to face the day when curtain falls. Please treasure your family love, love for your spouse, love for your friends. Treat everyone well and stay friendly with your neighbors.

All Media, Vibes

While we focus on educating our children with moral and humanistic values we need to demand from our current leaders love of humanity, social justice and the pursuit of peace. Discourage those persons who engage in hate and divisive speech and indulge in pursuit of power and exploitation of others. **Right now there is technology available to resolve peacefully and without violence intra-psychic, interpersonal, organizational, national and international conflicts.**

For further details see Selected Bibliography I Freedom From Oneself. Page 105.

3. Freedom from Religious Oppression: Most organized religions pursue money and power to promote their sectarian interests. For the most part religious leaders have betrayed their spiritual guides. The spiritual guides throughout history and across the continents shared their spiritual wisdom for everyone. All of these spiritual guides emphasized love as the path to realize the divine within us. But as their followers we create lists of people we should hate. **We should claim their wisdom as a human heritage like we do with developments in other fields of human endeavor.** If they said love thy neighbor as thyself it is not only the neighbor of a certain religion, caste or ethnicity. If they said there is a cosmic spiritual unity and inter-dependence of all creation it is not meant for just a certain segment of society. We should explore words of the spiritual guides and incorporate their wisdom in common into our academic curriculum as a humanistic, moral or civic sense curriculum.

4. Media: Communication is to Enhance Mutual Understanding: We need to minimize "symbolic interactions" based on preconceived notions of being liberals, conservatives, progressives and all other

kinds of ideologies and political parties or ethnic identities. If we are already attached to our preconceived notions then a constructive dialogue is impossible. We need to focus on using observable descriptive data and how these can be useful in problem solving instead of trying to score a victory of our preconceived position through manipulation of people through power, money and propaganda. We need to train our next generation not to think using stereotypes promoted by our leaders for the vested interests of the few. The media in almost every country is a propaganda tool. It promotes party, sectarian and national, corporate or religious interests. It does not represent the global humanistic viewpoint: fostering the wellbeing of all humanity.

For details refer to Selected Bibliography IV. Media Page 108.

5. Discrepancy between the Public Interest and Leadership Agenda: In Section VI The Populace Experience in Did India and Pakistan Win Freedom, you will notice that it contained a lot of wisdom and aspirations and is quite different from what the leaders settled upon among themselves.

For further details refer to Selected Bibliography II. India's Freedom Struggle. Page 107.

We need to stop hero worship of political personalities and challenge their pursuit of misconceived, vested interests in the name of patriotism or religion. Our need to put our leaders on a pedestal, as we did in India's freedom struggle, can lead us astray. We should evaluate leaders in terms of their interest in peace, harmony and humanistic values. As we know even the most famous and infamous leaders have had their merits and flaws. We know about Hitler but even the leaders who are Nobel laureates and had appreciation from their followers like Churchill are also credited with flaws.

The Crimes of Winston Churchill: Churchill was a genocidal maniac but is fawned over in Britain and held up as a hero of the nation. History however reveals the true face of Winston Churchill.

Afghanistan 1888: In Afghanistan he said that those who resisted would be killed without quarter, because the Pushtoons needed to recognize the superiority of race.

We proceeded systematically, village by village, and we destroyed the houses, filled up the walls, cut down the shady trees, burned the crops and broke the reservoirs in punitive devastation.

South Africa 1897: Thousands were sent to British-run concentration camps during the Boar war. Churchill summarized his time in South Africa by saying, "It was great fun galloping about." In June, 1916, Churchill argued that Afrikaner should be allowed self-rule, which would mean black people would be excluded from voting.

Palestine 1917: Churchill regarded Palestinians to be a "lower manifestation." And that "dogs in a manger has the final right to the manger." Churchill stated that he believed in the intention of the Balfous Declaration to make Palestine an overwhelming Jewish state.

Saudi Arabia 1922: He described Ibn Saud's Wahhabis as intolerant, well-armed and blood-thirsty, and said, "my admiration for him (Ibn Saud) was deep because of his unfailing loyalty to us." Prior to 1922 the British were paying Ibn Saud 60,000 pounds a year. Churchill, then the Colonial Secretary, raised it to 100,000 pounds.

Iraq 1920: In the 1920's various groups in the region rose up against the British. Under the direction of Churchill, the air force was put into action and indiscriminately bombed civilian areas. Churchill advised "the provision of some kind of 'asphyxiating' bombs for use in preliminary operations against turbulent tribes in order to take control of Iraq."

India 1943: Churchill said, "I hate Indians. They are beastly people with a beastly religion." His hatred for India led to four million people starving to death during the Bengal famine of 1943. The British Army took millions of tons of rice from starving people and Churchill rationalized "It was their fault for breeding like rats."

KIVIDS

As this article continues, in reference to Churchill, it describes a similar attitude and actions in Greece, Kenya and Iran.

The purpose of the above quotes is not to malign Churchill. The purpose is to appreciate his positive contributions but also learn from his mistakes that were motivated by a sectarian interest. Now we live in a global village and have to think and act according to our global interest and common humanity.

> **There is so much bad in the best of us**
>
> **And so much good in the worst of us,**
>
> **That it makes it tough on some of us**
>
> **To diagnose the rest of us**

William Tarnower. M.D.
Psychoanalyst

6. Multinational Corporations: The East India Trading Company was just one global company that wreaked havoc in India. Now we have to cope with many multinational corporations. These corporations have destroyed neighborhood family businesses, family farms and local industries for their profit. They are destroying the public education institutions. They have destroyed human relationships and cultures. Money has become the measure of all things. They control the United States Congress through their lobbyists and money. Legislative actions are taken to promote their interests and not the interest of the people. The gap between rich and the poor is not accidental. The congress enacted laws that promoted the interests of those who fund the campaigns for officials to come into power. Even the Supreme Court of the United States has ruled that giving money to the politicians is free speech. What a travesty! Previously, "money speaks" was a derogatory phrase. It is used to be that an action that was taken due to pursuasion by money (from those with the ability to pay) was considered a bribe.

There are institutions like World Bank and the International Monetary Fund (IMF) that serve their interests. These corporations are non-democratic. They can sue governments if they impede their profits. These corporations take no responsibility for polluting the environment and causing poverty among workers. We need to reign in these institutions if we want to save this planet and live in peace.

For more details refer to the Selected Bibliography VI. The Economic Gap Page 110.

In conclusion, practice the unity of human kind. Fortunately we have come a long way. There are institutions that already exist such as the International Criminal Court, various organizations within the United Nations and non-governmental organizations to promote goals like human rights, We need to support them and create more to promote love, peace and prosperity for all.

For further details please see Selected Bibliography I. Freedom From Oneself on the next page.

Selected Bibliography

I. Freedom From Oneself

If one wants to bring about socio-economic-political-spiritual change it has to begin with oneself. One has to learn from the spiritual guides (Not necessarily religions). They came from time to time to show us the way of personal transformation through love of the Creator, preserving and serving Its Creation and humanity, while reducing our attachment to greed, pride, sexual lust and anger. You may study such literature where you grew up and seek the company of persons who are pursuing their personal transformation to find support and encouragement to continue this arduous journey. I share with you what has been most helpful to me.

1. The Bible Handbook (1993), Thomas Nelson Publishers, Nashville, Tennessee, U.S.A.

2. Dev, Sri Guru Arjan (1604), Sri Guru Granth Sahib (Punjabi and Indian languages), Published by Shiromni Gurdwara Prabhndhak Committee, Amritsar, Punjab, India. Sri Guru Arjan Dev ji (1563-1606) was the fifth Guru of the Sikhs. He collected the poetical verses of the five Gurus and twenty-nine other Bhagats, Sufis and saints from different religions, castes, varying in social status and who were residents of different states in India. He edited this sacred book of 1430 pages; identifying the authors, the poetical form and the Ragas that were appropriate for singing these verses. The poetry of the Ninth Guru Tegh Bahadur ji, was added to the book by the tenth Guru, Sri Guru Gobind Singh ji , who transferred the final Guruship to Sri Granth Sahib. The poetry is full of love for the Divine Creator and appreciation of Its Creation. It repudiates superficial rituals and attachment to material pursuits that are necessary but not the goal of life. It emphasizes that we are all children of the same Creator and therefore equal. Further, we are to love each other, make an honest living and share it with persons in need. To maintain the loving devotion to the Creator and Its Creation one has to study and contemplate on Gurbani (Guru's words as expressed in their verses) and meditate every day. That will help reduce attachment to sexual lust, anger, greed, pride and pursuit of excessive material goods and foster love and awareness of spiritual unity of life on this planet.

3. Gurbani Researcher, International Institute of Gurmat Studies, 1930 Francisco Way, Richmond, Ca., U.S.A., www.IIGS.Com support@ IIGS.com. This one CD makes it is easy to search any verse in Sri Guru Granth Sahib and find its English translation.

4. Harari, Y.N. (2015), Sapiens; A Brief History of Human Kind, Harper Collins Publishers, 195 Broadway, New York, N.Y. 10007. One hundred thousand years ago, at least six human species inhabited the earth. Today there is just one. How did our species succeed to dominate? Why did our foraging ancestors come together to create cities and kingdoms? How did we come to believe in gods, nations, and human rights; to trust money, timetables and consumerism? What will our world be like in the millennia to come?

5. Keay, John (2000), India, A History, Grove Press, New York

6. Macauliffe, Max Arthur (1978), S. Chand & Company Ltd. Ram Nagar, New Delhi – 110055, India. Six volume history of Sikhs

7. Quran Majeed (Urdu), Urdu Translation and interpretation by Maulana Ashraf Ali Sahib Thanvi, Fareed Book Store, Jaama Masjid, Delhi

8. The Holy Quran, English Translation of the Meanings and Commetary, (1411 H), King Fahd Holy Quran Printing Complex, P.O. Box 3561Al-Madinah Al-Munawarah, Saudi Arabia

9. Radhakrishnan (Revised Edition 1931), 2 volumes. New York: The Macmillan Company London: George Allen & Unwin Ltd. Dr. Radhakrishnan was a Professor of Indian Philosophy and the second President of Free India. These two volumes give a history of the emergence of Indian thought and its relationship to Indian religions and life and its' socio-cultural and political implications. It begins with the Vedic period and includes the two epics Mahabharta and Ramayana plus everything you have ever heard about Indian concepts. You have heard about different religions, such as Buddhism, Jainism and a variety of Indian thought and practices, such as Yoga and Materialism. These volumes are nearly an historical encyclopedia of Indian philosophy.

10. Schwartz, Michael, Director (2002) Muhammad: Legacy of A Proph-

et, Kikim Media, 887 Oakgrove Avenue, Suite 201, Menlo Park, California, 94025

11. Swami Sivnand (1995), Bhagvad Gita, The Divine Lfe Society, P.O. Shivananda Nagar -249 192, Distt. Tehri Garwal, U.P. Himalayas, India

12. Zinn, Howard People's History of he United States Read by Matt Damon and Howard Zinn, www.Harperaudio.com.

13. Stone, Oliver, (2013), Untold History of the United States, 12 chapters on 4 DVD Discs, Warner Brothers Inc.

II. India's Freedom Struggle

1. Azad, Abul Kalam (1988), India Wins Freedom, Orient Blackswan Private Limited, 1/24 Asaf Ali Road, New Delhi 110 002. It is the story of India's freedom struggle narrated by the insider who spent all his life in India's struggle for freedom, was once the President of Indian National Congress and had very close relationships with the Congress leadership.

2. Hajari, N.(2015) Midnight's Furies, Houghton Miffin, Harcourt Publishing Company, 215 Park Ave. South, New York, New York 10003. Midnight's Furies relies on fresh historical sources to go beyond the familiar debate about Hindus and Muslims were at odds over the future of India, and shows how decisions by leaders reacting to unfolding events sealed the fate of united India and produced the cycle of violence that forever marked the peoples and governments of the region. Well researched and eminently readable, this haunting account puts into the proper perspective both history and current events. VALI NASR of the Shiva Revival Chapter - III

3. Sidhwa, B. (1991), Cracking India, a novel, Milkweed Editions, 1011 Washington Ave. South, Suite 300, Minneapolis, Minnesota, 55415. It is a historical novel describing the tragedy of partition through the ordinary characters in Lahore. It reveals not only the tragedy of partition of a country but the psychological trauma of the victims of this partition- a humanistic novel. This was made into an award winning movie Earth directed by Deepa Mehta

4. Zakaria, Rafia (2015) The Upstairs Wife: An Intimate History of Pakistan, Beacon Press, Boston, Massachusetts. Rafia discusses complex strands of Pakistan history, from the problematic colonialism to the terrorist violence to increasing misogyny, interweaving them with arc of her aunt Amina's life to reveal the toll Pakistan's increasing conservatism has taken on its women.

III. Political Economics

1. Kelso Louis O. and Kelso, Patricia Hetter Power, University Press of America, Lanham, New York, London

2. Singh, J.P. (1999) Leap Frogging Development? The Political Economy of Telecommunications Restructuring, State University of New York Press, State University Plaza, Albany, N.Y., 12246

3. Singh, J.P. (2008) Negotiation And The Global Information Economy, Cambridge University Press, Cambridge, U.K.

4. Singh, J.P. (2011) Globalized Arts The Entertainment Economy And Cultural Identity, Columbia University Press, New York

5. Singh, J.P. (2017) Sweet Talk Paternalism And Collective Action In North-South Trade Relations, Stanford University Press, Stanford, California

6. Smith, J.W. (2000) Economic Democracy: The Political Struggle of the Twenty-first Century, M.E. Sharpe, Armonk, New York, London, England

7. Stiglitz, Joseph E. (2002) Globalization and Its Discontents, W.W. Norton & Company, New York London

8. Ziv, Ilan (2013) Capitalism A Six-Part Series, Icarus Films, 32 Court Street, 21st. Floor, Brooklyn, N.Y. 11201

IV. Media

1. Chomsky, Noam, Two-part VHS video, National Film Board of Canada. Part One Thought Control in a Democracy. Part Two Activating Discussion

2. Cohen, Jeff and Solomon, Norman (1995) Through the Media Looking Glass: Decoding Bias and Blather in the news, common Courage Press, Box 702 Monroe, ME 04951

3. MacArthur, John R. (1993) Second Front Censorship And Propaganda in the Gulf War, University of California Press, Berkeley, Los Angeles, London

4. Phillips, Peter & Project Censored (2003) Censored 2004: The top 25 censored stories, Seven Stories Press, 140 Watts Street, New York, N.Y. 10013

5. Singh, Michael (2015) Valentino's Ghost: The politics Behind Images, www.valentenosghost.com, Michael Singh Productions, Inc. (323)466-5000

V. Interventions and Regime Change

1. Chatterji, Pratap (2004) Iraq, Inc. A Profitable Occupation, Seven Stories Press, 140 Watts Street, New York, N.Y. 10013

2. Dreyfuss, Robert (2005) Devil's Game: How the United States Helped Unleash Fundamentalist Islam, Henry Holt and Company, LLC, 175 Fifth Avenue, New York, N.Y.10010

3. Fisk, Robert (2005) The Great War Of Civilization: The Conquest of the Middle East, Alfred A. Knopf, New York 2006

4. Galeano, Eduardo (1997), Open Veins of Latin America, Monthly Review Press, New York

5. Getzel, Peter and Lopez, Eduardo, Directors, Based on the book by Journalist Juan Gonzalez (2012), Harvest of Empire, www.harvestofempiremovie.com

6. Kinzer, Stephen (2006) Overthrow: America's Century of Regime Change from Hawaii to Iraq, Henry Holt and Company, LLC, 175 Fifth Avenue, New York, N.Y.10010

7. Kirby, John, Director (2007) The American Ruling Class, bullfrogfilms, PO Box 149, Oley, PA 19547

8. Pappe, Ilan (2006), The Ethnic Cleansing of Palestine, Oneworld Publications Limited, 185 Banbury Road, Oxford OX27AR, England

9. Moyers, Bill (1987) The Secret Government – The Constitution in Crisis, Public Affairs Television, 356 West 58th Street, New York, N.Y.10019

10. Perkins, John (2004) Confessions of an Economic Hit Man, Berrett-Kohler Publishers, 235 Montgomery Street Pizzot, Suite 650, San Francisco, Ca. 94104

11. Scahill, Jeremy , Dirty Wars: A Secret Army, A War Without End. A Journalist Determined to Uncover the Truth, Civic Bakery DVD

12. Stone, Oliver (2010) South of the Border, Cinema Libre Studio, www.cinemalibrestudio.com

13. Z, A Film by Costa-Gavras (1967) in French with English subtitles

14. The Crisis of civilization, a film by Dean Puckett, www.crisisofcivilization.com

VI. The Economic Gap Between the Rich and Poor is Intentional, Cruel and Dangerous:

1. Causey, Francis and Goldmacher, Donald (2012) Heist: Who Stole the American Dream?, A Feature Documentary, 2012 Connecting the Dots Productions, LLC

2. Chomsky, Noam (2015) Requiem For the American Dream, FilmRise Color DVD

3. Chomsky, Noam (2006) Failed State: The Abuse of Power and Assault on Democracy, Penguin Books Ltd., 80 Strand, London WC2R ORL England

4. Danaher, Kevin (1994) 50 Years Is Enough: The Case Against the World Bank and the International Monetary Fund, South End Press, Boston, MA

5. Goodman, Amy (2004) The Exception to the Rulers, Hyperion, 77 West 66th Street, New York, N.Y. 10023

6. Johnston, David Cay (2003) Perfectly Legal: The Covert Campaign to Rig Our Tax System to Benefit the Super Rich – And Cheat Everybody Else, Penguin Group (U.S.A.) Inc.375 Huds0n Street, New York, N.Y.10014 U.S.A.

7. Johnston, David Cay (2007) Free Lunch: How the Wealthiest Americans Enrich Themselves At Government Expense (And Stick You the Bill) Penguin Group (U.S.A.) Inc., 375 Hudson Street, New York, N.Y.10014 U.S.A.

8. Korten, David C. (1995) When Corporations Rule the World, Kumarian Press Inc.630 Oakwood Avenue, Suite 119, West Hartford, Connecticut 06110, U.S.A. and Berrett-Koehler Publishers Inc. 155 Montgomery Street, San Francisco, California, 94104

9. McLean, Bethany and Elkind, Peter (2004) The Smartest Guys in the Room: The Amazing Rise And Scandalous Fall of Enron, Penguin Group (U.S.A.), 375 Hudson Street, New York, New York 10014 U.S.A.

10. Park Avenue DVD, Money, Power and the American Dream

11. Pizzo, Stephen, Fricker, Mary & Muolo, Paul (1991) Inside Job: The Looting of America's Savings and Loans, Harper Collins Publishers, 10 East 53rd. Street, New York, N.Y. 10022

12. Reich, Robert (2013) Inequality For All, The Western Company DVD, www.anchorbayent.com

13. Risen, James (2014) Pay Any Price: Greed, Power, and endless War, Houghton Miffin Harcourt Publishing Company, 215 Park Avenue South, New York 10003

14. Waring, Marilyn (1995) Who's Counting: Sex, Lies and Global Economics, Produced by the National Film Board of Canada, Suite B, Director: Terry Nash, Producer: Kent Martin

15. Wolff, Richard D. (2010), Capitalism Hits the Fan: The Global Economic Meltdown and what to do about it, Interlink Publishers Group, Inc., 46 Crosby Street, Northampton, MA

16. Death in the West, Pyramid Film and Video, Box 1048, Santa Moni-

ca, CA 90406

VII. Awakening and Hope

1. An Avi Lewis Film (2015?) This Changes Everything. www.this-changeseverything.org

2. Galleymore, Susan (2009) Long Time Passing: Mothers Speak About War and Terror, Pluto Press345 Archway Road, London N6 SAA and 175 Fifth Avenue, New York, N.Y..10010

3. Goodman, Amy and Moynihan, Denis (2012) The Silenced Majority: Stories of Uprisings, Occupations, Resistance, And Hope, Haymarket Books, P.O. Box180165, Chicago, IL. 60618

4. Kitchel, Mark, a film (2012) A Fierce Green Fire: The Battle for a Green Planet, www.forstrunfeatures.com

5. Kline, Naomi (2007) The Shock Doctrine: The Rise of Disastrous Capitalism, Henry Holt and Company, 175 Fifth Avenue, New York, NY 10001

6. Moore, Michael (2016) Where to Invade Next: Prepare to be Liberated, Star Media LLC

7. Palast, Greg (2016) The Best Democracy Can Buy: A Tale of Billionaires and Bandits, Cinema Libre

8. Wachowski Brothers, V for Vendetta, Warner Brothers Films

9. Orwell, George (1949) 1984, a Novel, New American Library, a Division of Penguin Group (USA), 175 Hudson Street, New York, N.Y. 10014. After President Trump's election, George Orwell'a 1984 became a best seller again. Media commentators thought that much of what 1984 said is coming true now. I beg to differ with them. We have been living the nightmare of George Orwell's fiction all this time but we were asleep. Trump has woken us up. I note a few examples from 1984:

- In the novel the ministry of love specialized in torture: Study our criminal justice system and the use of torture for political purposes through the 20th century up to the early 21st. century.

- The ministry for truth altered facts. Who controls the past controls the future. Who controls present controls the past: Study history of any country. It supports the view of the ruling class. Only recently are there historical narratives from victim's point of view. Most citizens still live in patriotic fervor and do not pursue humanistic values.

- The Party controls the record and the memory: Any one who differs from the party establishment is demonized such as Bernie Sanders. Any one who reveals truth is persecuted by the ruling elite. Whistle blowers are are unthanked and even persecuted for revealing the truth. President Obama prosecuted more whistle blowers than prior presidents put together.

- Reality resides in human mind and is in the mind of the Party not in the individual. The commercial media has promoted ruling class interests and supported wars under false pretext.

- Perennial Wars. Under the guise of national interest, enemies are created to foster arms trade to benefit the vested interest of the few. Now we have a perennial war against terrorism. All this has been going on before Trump. Now people have caught up with it around the world.

Chapter - III

A TRAGIC WAKE UP CALL

September, 2001

The deeper the sleep the harder it is to awake. For thousands of years we have created a nightmare of a civilization based upon an unworkable paradigm of power, greed and violence in the service of misconceived self-interest. In spite of the untold suffering it has caused throughout history, we have not questioned this paradigm. The promise of a good material life and the pomp and propaganda of the power elite have lulled us to sleep time and again. The horrific tragedy of September 11th; 2001, the attack on the World Trade Center in New York, the Pentagon in Washington and the plane crash in Pennsylvania has shaken us out of our slumber. Usually, the response is to take quick action that may be necessary. We are also provided with an opportunity for reflection and to make some basic changes in the way we conduct ourselves in relationship to each other and other nations. The roots of such a destructive civilization can be illustrated by the following biblical story.

There were two brothers named Abel and Cain. **Abel (Naam consciousness)** loved God. He was a selfless, loving and caring individual. He did not care about material possessions. He would serve his fellow humans and share with them. In return everyone loved him. On the other hand his brother **Cain (Haumain consciousness)** was self-centered, greedy and jealous. He hankered after worldly possessions. He was disliked. He was so full of rage and anger that he killed his loving brother and buried him. When God discovered this horrific deed he put a mark on Cain's forehead and banished him. **Cain established the first city, the beginning of our modern civilization. Ever since we have been living in Cain consciousness.**

From time to time God-loving beings have appeared in different parts of this planet to revive the Abel consciousness but the power elite of the time buried them again and again. No sooner were they buried, some of us, even in the name of these loving beings, performed horrific deeds. Possessed by Cain consciousness, some of us forgot the true message of these spiritual guides.

Jesus Christ was the embodiment of love. He loved all his fellow human beings regardless of their status or lot in life. He protected the woman who was labeled as a sinner by societal judges. He was murdered by a collaboration of the clergy and the Roman ruling class. He forgave the people who brutally murdered him. After his death Romans co-opted his name and became "Christians." They did not incorporate his love. It was a ploy to maintain their power. They did not dismantle their armies or abandon their greed and lust for power. Ever since, to date, the power elite in different countries have murdered and plundered in Christ's name.

Hazrat Muhammad preached the divine love of one God and equality among fellow human beings. The power elite in Mecca, comprised of the ruling class, business owners and clergy, tried to murder him but he escaped to Medina. Nevertheless a vast majority of Arabs were touched by his message. He walked back into Mecca with his followers without any arms. Later the power elite, in the name of Muhammad, murdered and plundered in different parts of the world.

From Guru Nanak through Guru Gobind Singh, the ten Gurus brought a message of divine love. They taught the alleviation of Haumain ("I am" consciousness) through meditation. This meditation was to achieve Abel consciousness, realize the Divine Creator in oneself and to perceive the Divine in Its creation. Their hope was to serve the Divine by preserving Its creation and serving humanity. The followers have ended their morning and evening meditations with the prayer, "by the grace of the Divine, let there be wellbeing of every one." The Mughal Empire in collaboration with local Hindu Rajas and Muslim governors murdered two out of the ten Gurus. Another Guru died fighting to protect the unprotected. Yet some of us possessed by Haumain (Cain) consciousness have become quite sectarian.

We have been so numbed by Cain (Haumain) consciousness that we demonize and dehumanize our fellow human beings and mercilessly murder them to rob them of their resources for our personal profit. Do you have a child you love? Think of that child and reflect upon the following:

Sometime last year journalist Leslie Stahl interviewed our Secretary of State Madam Albright. Stahl brought to her attention some United Nations' statistics. By that time five hundred thousand children had died because of our sanctions against Iraq. She asked Madam Albright, is the death of five hundred thousand children worth it? Her answer was that, considering everything, it was worth it. Can you imagine if one of the dead was your child and what this means to the child's mother, father, brothers, sisters, cousins, friends, uncles, aunts and grandparents. One child's death affects so many people. Imagine what the death of a half-million children does to a country. They were all civilians. They had done no harm to any one of us.

We lost over five thousand (the original published figure) innocent American lives at the World Trade Center. So far I have met no one who did not know of someone who perished in the New York tragedy or was unaffected by it in some way. It has impacted all of us. By this time there must be a million innocent civilians who have perished because of our sanctions. We keep bombing Iraq. Calling it collateral damage, we have destroyed millions of lives. What do you think is the impact on that nation? There are scores of countries in Latin America, Asia and Africa where our National Security Agency has helped to destroy millions of lives.

There is a small minority among us who remain touched by such trag-edies. The rest of us have been lulled to sleep by the press and the politi-cians. The (first) Iraqi war has brought neither democracy to Kuwait nor prosperity to the States. Since then there are more homeless people and fewer resources for health, education and welfare. The gap between the rich and the poor is widening. Who profited from such murders? Wake up and think hard. Five hundred thousand and millions of other civilian lives, as innocent as the thousands of fellow American civilians killed on September 11, have been ended abruptly in horrific tragedy.

"Eternal vigilance is the price of democracy." We have been ill informed by our press, which serves the power elite and not the people of the United States. A free press is the conscience of a country. The corpora-tions have bought our main news media. The person who pays the piper calls the tune. In addition to the daily selective reporting, the latest blatant betrayal of the public trust by the press is the covenant among the five major T.V. news networks and the state department. It defined what they would and would not report. The British Prime Minister, Tony Blair, made a similar request of the B.B.C. news network and they refused. There is an all out effort to silence the only alternative radio in the States. Senator Robert Dole declared the KPFA radio station as a hate broadcaster. They have no interest in its mission, which is to promote peace and provide commercial free, objective reporting of news and culture. It is ominous to curb free dissemination of information and dissent.

Since passage of the National Security Act in 1947, giving birth to the National Security Agency, the American public has been duped repeatedly with false propaganda in the name of national security. I cannot forget Colonel North's testimony before the Senate Committee hearings regarding the Iran Contra affair. The Senate Committee counsel asked Col. North was he not shocked that he had an "off the shelf" army that could make unilateral decisions to destabilize foreign governments and lie to Congress. Col. North proudly said, "No Sir." He said that he was being a patriot. According to him we live in a dangerous world and cannot trust the U.S. Congress. If he shared information with Congress he believed it would be leaked. The counsel reminded him that by his own testimony the Russians already had the information. So he was keeping secrets only from the people of the United States. He had literally subverted the U.S. Constitution. This is being done again.

We, the people of the United States are not fully informed. Out of all the Congress members, there was only one who voted to protect the Constitution. She did not want to give President Bush unlimited war powers without congressional oversight. Weeks later when President Bush sent a memo to withhold intelligence information from otherwise appropriate members of the Congress, did Congress react furiously to the withholding of information? Nevertheless, the single courageous Congresswoman Barbara Lee was misrepresented and maligned by the media and received death threats. In the name of the National Security and patriotism, attempts are made to encroach upon the civil rights of citizens and freedom of speech.

It is not patriotic to follow our leaders blindly. As responsible citizens we need to inform ourselves and question our leaders. History is replete with leaders misleading their people and creating untold destruction and suffering. It is especially true when our leaders are motivated by Cain consciousness.

Any leader who perpetuates hatred against any group of people or countries and tries to justify violence to solve political problems is promoting Cain consciousness. You may be aware of the fact that it is against the United Nations charter to invade another country. You can fight to defend yourself. Violence has never solved any problem in the history of humankind. Even those people who are working toward peace, but are abusive toward the people they disagree with, are not promoting peace. We have to come from a place of love otherwise we are still acting in Cain consciousness and that will not promote peace. Leaving aside the great spiritual beings like Christ, Muhammad, Budha and Nanak, I give you an example of an incident that happened in Oakland, California a couple of weeks ago.

A few young men intoxicated by patriotic fervor and revenge walked into a store owned by a Muslim shopkeeper. They roughed up the man and made a mess of his store. Someone called the police. The police arrested the young men and asked the storeowner if he wanted to press charges. He declined. The police let the men go. The same young men returned to the store that evening. They put his stuff in the store in place, apologized and gave him money for the things they had broken. The storekeeper acted in Abel consciousness and revived Abel in the young men. Love begets love! What are our leaders and Osama Bin Laden doing? Could you guess what is their consciousness? Who or what do you support?

It is time to realize the interconnectedness and interdependence of the whole universe. The mystics of all faiths realized this thousands of years ago. Ecological studies show how the tiniest creatures on this planet, the forests and remote habitats sustain the delicate balance of life. When we destroy any part of this planet we destroy a part of ourselves. When we use depleted uranium to bomb any country, it spreads radiation around the planet. The Russians never attacked us with nuclear weapons. Our nuclear tests and chemical pollution have increased cancer rates fourfold during the last three decades.

The power elite, that includes political, business, academic, religious leaders and the media in every country is driven by Cain consciousness and has created a paranoid civilization. Everyone learns in introductory psychology courses that paranoid ideation is a projection of one's anger. Anger is a result of a feeling of being hurt. The paranoid person can develop an elaborate delusional system to justify his/her distrust of other people. In a psychotic rage the paranoid person can unleash all the power in his/her possession to destroy the perceived enemy. **Beneath**

this anger lies intense pain and suffering inflicted upon the person while he/she was a helpless child. It is the healing of that pain that re-establishes trust and rekindles love in the person. We need to initiate a healing process to alleviate the pain that we have inflicted upon each other for thousands of years. No one trusts any one. We are still building bigger and better bombs and missile defense systems. These will make a lot of money for a few at the expense of the rest of humanity. It serves no humane purpose. We need to wake up and shake off the nightmare we have been living in because of self-centered, hateful Cain consciousness.

There is a highly developed conflict resolution technology available to resolve conflicts in a peaceful manner. It is not going to be easy to change hateful paranoid consciousness and utilize peaceful conflict resolution. But recognition of a problem and the willingness to solve that problem is the first step toward liberating ourselves from this nightmare of suffering. In my experience as an organizational development consultant it takes a similar process of unconditional loving investment in the organization and setting aside value judgments on the manifest behavior of the individuals in the organization that brings about positive change.

We, the people in each country can demand from our political, business, academic, religious and media elite that they promote peaceful conflict resolution by asking for available technical help. It will cost a pittance compared to the defense budgets of each country that bring nothing but suffering. Politically we should encourage the power elite to promote planetary justice by supporting the International Criminal Court, reducing global warming, preserving forests, supporting population control, disarmament and fair trade, not free trade. Our elite need to encourage payment of a proper price for the purchase of the resources from different countries instead of plunder them by violent force. They should promote a just economic system devoid of exploitation of others for misconceived self-interest.

Does it sound like a utopia? Does it sound like an unachievable goal? Compare it to the utopia we are living in now. It is a complete utopia to think that a person, a community or a nation can live in peace by exploiting others. We have not given up this utopian thinking in the face of a preponderance of evidence that it has brought nothing but wars, suffering and perpetual misery. **The tragic events of September 11th have**

amply demonstrated that power and violence does not protect us. We have a choice to give up our hateful and paranoid delusional thinking and replace it with love and caring.

Cain and Abel are within us. It is a constant struggle within each of us to keep Abel alive. In spite of my life long struggle to live in Abel consciousness through spiritual practice, professional discipline and understanding of psychological processes, Cain shows up whenever I am under emotional pressure. The latest example is the varied reactions I had during the past few weeks. I was in New York when on a perfectly beautiful day the tragedy began to unfold at the World Trade Center. Soon after I began to listen to President Bush's statements: We are going to punish the terrorists and the countries that harbor the terrorists. It is war between good and evil. It is a crusade to destroy the terrorist network. It is operation Infinite Justice. Either you are with us or against us.

The press coverage was totally devoid of political analysis. I felt helpless, angry, frustrated and depressed. What happened to my loving consciousness?

By Saturday of the same week I managed to get back to California. I returned to the company of my colleagues who practice unconditional love and acceptance of patients who suffer from major mental illness. We stay focused on the pain and suffering and avoid enmeshment in the manifest behavior. We see their behavior as their own solution to their pain and unmanageable anxiety. We approach the same way when we consult with an organization. We focus on the pressures impinging on the organization and do not make value judgments on the manifest behavior of the individuals. It is the **interaction** with the psychotherapist or consultant who is seeking to understand with compassion that brings about change. With the support of my colleagues and peace loving friends, I began to look at the pressures on the President. It was the unforeseen attack upon the very heart of modern civilization. There is an intense hurt and pain because of the tragic losses. There is a fear and anxiety because of the unseen perpetrator. There is the historic conditioning of solving political problems with violence. The President has the responsibility to alleviate and help cope with all this. Observing in this way promotes more compassion for the President. **Even though, I still believe that he is using a non-productive, habitual way to respond to such a horrific tragedy. His administration needs a lot of help before**

they destroy life on this planet.

This essay as well as my continued involvement with my friends in the interfaith and peace promoting community is my attempt to deal with my sense of helplessness and desperation that I experience as I witness repeatedly the tragedy of a misdirected human civilization. Bringing about change is not an intellectual process. It requires time for the patient pursuit of compassionate understanding and the support of others to prevent becoming Cain. Intellectual awareness helps us to begin the effort toward positive change.

May the Divine bless our planet and its inhabitants with Love and Peace!

Our home, Sweet home!

6-11-17 Post Script:

This article was written in October, 2001. A lot has happened since Nine-Eleven. I saw Osama Bin Laden on CNN on October 6, 2001. After that, President Bush banned televising him out of concern that he might use American television to transmit hidden messages for the sleeping cells of Al Qaida in the U.S. I remember that Bin Laden made the following three points against the United States:

1. After Osama returned to Saudi Arabia, and his participation in the withdrawal of the Russians from Afghanistan, he found that the United States was planning to attack Iraq and use Saudi Arabia as the base. He objected to the American Army being stationed on Saudi soil on religious grounds. Mecca is the holiest place for Muslims. The American living style is contrary to Muslims. Muslims do not drink alcohol and drinking is a part of the Army's habits of consumption. Osama felt that if he, with the support of the Arabs, could defeat the Russians, they could take care of Saddam without an American presence. He ended up in exile in Sudan.

2. The West had a history of supporting dictatorships in Arab countries that had no interest in the wellbeing of their own people.

3. The West's unconditional support of Israel against the Palestinians.

You might disagree with him but you cannot call him evil. You cannot make up your own explanation that "he hates our freedom" as the U.S. governmental line was promoted in the press. Defined as evil, negotiation was not an option. Alas, with evil you can only destroy it.

The subsequent president and administration followed the same attitude, hunted him and murdered him.

1. President Bush and the Vice President took the country to war against Iraq on a false pretext and most of the commercial press supported him including the New York Times. ISIS is the direct result of it.

2. United States hawks always have to have some enemy to fight to support the military contractors. They wage a never-ending war on "Terrorism."

3. The civil rights of the citizen and freedom of speech are threatened by the Patriot Act.

4. President Trump is following the same policies in the Middle East and Iran. He is supporting the Saudi Kingdom and allying with Israel against Iran. Such divisiveness can never bring peace. President Obama tried to have a balanced policy regarding Middle East and Iran. But the Republicans hated any reconciliation or move toward peace.

Chapter - IV

Beyond Interfaith Dialogue

In 1996 I was invited to join a group to try out a workbook for interfaith dialogue. Our group represented several different religions. It was a part of the developmental process of the United Religions Initiative (URI). At the end of eight weeks Sally Mahe, the Director of Organizational Development for URI, came to receive feedback from the groups. Our group had two major findings to share:

1. To facilitate participation, creative action and a contribution to world peace, a hierarchical structure would not be useful. We recommended that URI not model its organizational structure after the United Nations hierarchical structure. We felt it would then become subject to the same kind of power struggle in choosing officers for the organization, such as, which office should be held by which religion. **The URI developed an ingenious organizational model.** It was non-hierarchical and more in line with the spiritual sentiment of service rather than authority. It is a wheel with a hub and connecting spokes linking all the inter-faith Co-operation Circles. The central office serves to connect the Cooperation Circles. These interfaith groups are quite autonomous, develop their own projects and have their own officers. At present there are over 400 such Cooperation Circles in over 70 countries connected to the hub office in San Francisco.

2. The challenge of convening, sustaining and bearing peaceful fruit is less within the context of inter-faith than it is within intra-faith. During this URI development demonstration, our group members had become very close friends. It was very easy to have interfaith dialogue with the group members. We found that most people who come to such groups are already open-minded. Our discovery is that **the problem is intra-faith. It was within our respective faith groups that we would have the most difficulty convincing persons that it is very desirable to respect other faiths.** We felt it was more difficult to have an intra-faith dialogue because each of the religions has a large population with a very egocentric view of themselves. For example: "The Jews are the chosen people." "If you do not accept Christ as your Savior you are going straight to hell and will be left behind on Judgment Day;" "The Sikhs

are the Pure ones;" and "Anyone who is not a Muslim is a non-believer Kafir or infidel." Hindus assert with pride that they are the most tolerant religion, forgetting their most oppressive caste system practice. Every religion consists of persons who are spiritually centered and altruistic and others who are motivated by power or fear. Some of them will not hesitate to use violence to promote their agenda. I have been preoccupied with this problem for a very long time: From the massacre of over a million people and the forced total migration of the population in Punjab during the partition of India in 1947 to the tragedy of September 11, 2001. The URI preamble states:

> **We, the people of diverse religions, spiritual expressions and indigenous traditions throughout the world, hereby establish the United Religions Initiative to promote enduring, daily interfaith cooperation, to end religiously motivated violence and to create cultures of peace, justice and healing for the earth and all living beings.**

On the basis of my experience I have come to the following conclusions regarding **religiously motivated violence:**

1. There has never been any religiously motivated violence in human history. **The religions have been used by the power elite (ruling and business class, clergy and media) of the time to achieve its political goals. The spiritual essence of each religion is totally distorted by the power elite in order to achieve its misconceived vested interests. It is important to make this distinction.** To solve a problem one needs to define the problem accurately so that the interventions can be targeted accurately and reach more effective solutions.

2. As a clinical psychologist, I know that change in deeply held unconscious belief systems does not occur through intellectual discourse. The change occurs by unconditional acceptance and a non-judgmental and non-reactive presence. Further, it is how the clinician listens and responds to the reality that the patient creates in relationship to the therapist. Such unconditional acceptance gradually helps to get a person detached from the past programming that occurs in one's formative years. It takes weeks, months and sometimes years to accomplish such change. To undo the attachment we have as individuals, communities and nations, with a history of human civilization based upon egotistical motives, it takes a lot more effort than writing an essay. **In an organi-**

zational context I have been able to help participants to detach from their preconceived solutions with a consultation methodology that I have developed based on Professor Gerald Caplan, M.D.'s Theory and Practice of Mental Health Consultation. My main purpose in writing this essay is to bring to the attention of the power elite that there is another way of looking at problems and introduce the fact that now there is technology available to the power elite to employ more appropriate and peaceful techniques of conflict management instead of misconceived self-interest in service of our common survival on this planet.

3. The basic conflict is between the self-centered motivation to dominate and exploit others for personal interests versus the spiritual motivation that springs from love and self-surrender in the service of others. It plays out within each individual and reflects itself in community, religious or national interest. In every religion there are people who incorporate the loving spiritual aspect of their religion and others who incorporate the self-centered power motivated aspect of their religion. **We must revive within ourselves and our communities and nations aspects that reduce the misconceived personal or national interest. We must try to liberate ourselves from attachment to the idea that I am better than everyone else, my religion is better than other religions, my country is better than any other country, my economic theory or system of government is better than any other system and what I think is better than what you think. We need to listen to each other in a detached way instead of proving our point.**

I am going to start from the beginning of Judo-Christian-Islamic religions. Let me start with Moses. He could have been the most powerful person of his time as the Pharaoh of Egypt. **He chose to abdicate his power and with love, sided with suffering, oppressed humanity and liberated the slaves.** What did the power elite of the time do? His Pharaoh Brother pursued him to kill him and the slaves he liberated. Moses created the most humane Ten Commandments, including love thy neighbor as thyself. He did not say love only your Jewish neighbor. Following is an excerpt from Deuteronomy, a Jewish prayer for the blessing of a new home:

      And you shall love yourself

> **For you are a spark of the Divine**
>
> **And you shall love your neighbor as yourself**
>
> **And you shall love the stranger**
>
> **For you were strangers in the land of Egypt**
>
> **Let love fill your heart for all beings.**

The most disrespectful view of God is that God is just the God of Moses. Whatever name we use for the Creator that Creator is the Creator of this cosmos and is not confined to any one religion or sect.

Many of us know what the Israeli government is doing to its neighbors in the name of the Jewish religion. It smacks more of Pharaoh's imperial power than love of Moses for the oppressed humanity. It has nothing to do with Jewish spiritual practice. It is a very complex political problem and should be understood in that light. It has nothing to do with religion. The pretext of the security of Jewish state is mostly unfounded. As a psychologist I am more interested in the underlying processes than the overt statements. When I was in India about fifty years ago, during elections, the Sikh leaders would go to the villages and say, "The Panth (the Sikh community) is in danger. You must vote for the Panth." At that time I thought that these Sikh leaders exploiting the innocent villagers. Then I saw the same phenomenon in the most powerful and well-educated country in the world when President Reagan said that the security of the United States was threatened by Granada and invaded this tiny country. The same statement of threat to national security and appeal to patriotism was used by Hitler and has been used by many politicians in the world. **There are Jews, in and outside of Israel who have a different view than the Israeli government. The power elite uses fear to exploit its population and manipulates with emotionally charged concepts such as patriotism, community or religion to achieve its political goals.**

After Moses came Christ who tried to revive spiritual aspects of the religion and preached love and forgiveness. He even said, "Love your enemy." What did the power elite of that time did to him? The Pharisees and the Romans collaborated to murder him. After he was gone his followers created a religion in his name and the Romans adopted Christianity as the state religion. Did the Romans abandon violence? Did they stop killings and dismantle their armies? Instead they started killing in the name of Christ. The Vatican became a power center in itself. The history of Vatican is replete with power intrigues and murders. There have been spiritually motivated Christians who serve their fellow human beings with love.

In Europe we persecuted Jews for 2000 years. We tried to eradicate them and at last settled them in the Middle East and supported them to keep fighting with their Arab kith and kin. To this day we have continued killing in the name of Christ. Even today our President George Bush converted the political situation of Nine-Eleven tragedy into a religious "crusade" against "evil." The press became his mouthpiece. There was no political analysis of the anger of the Arab countries. The press accepted the formulation that there are axis of evil in this world and that we define where they are. We cannot negotiate with evil. We have to destroy it. At that time the service at the National Cathedral in Washington looked like the Roman power grandeur when all the five-star generals and the Presidents walked in a procession. It did not reflect Christ with his unconditional and undaunted love. Osama Bin Laden has used religion to rally Arabs to fight against U.S.S.R. and then the United States. For President Bush of the United States his major base emerges from the right wing Christian community. Even other Republican leaders, such as John McCain, have pointed out that the United States is a Christian country; not in spirit but for political purposes. McCain came out to protect Georgia (Formerly part of USSR) because it was one of the first countries that adopted Christianity.

Christ was followed by the Prophet Muhammad. He said that the slave and the master are the same. He brought the message of love of one God and that we should treat His creation also with love. He preached dialogue, not violence and brought unity among the warring Arab tribes. Following is one of the revelations of God to Prophet Muhammad as written in the Quran:

**O Mankind, we have created you from a
single (pair) of male and female**

And made you into nations and tribes

That ye may know each other

Not that ye may despise each other.

What did the power elite of his time do to him? The businessmen, the ruling class and the clergy of Mecca conspired to kill him. He was lucky that he escaped to Medina. He justified war only to defend oneself. But his followers created a religion to convert people with violence. The Christians and Muslims killed people to save their souls. They had Crusades and Jihads.

In the East in the Punjab State of India the Muslim Sufi poet saints and the Sikh Gurus, Guru Nanak through Guru Gobind Singh, brought a message of love and Cosmic Naam consciousness i.e., there is one Creator who manifests It Self in Its creation. Therefore, everything and everyone is sacred. Loving the Creator and serving Its creation is the way to merge with the Creator. It follows that you cannot discriminate against anyone on any grounds. India at that time was in the grips of a very rigid caste system. The Brahmins (the priestly caste), Kashtrya (warrior caste), Hindu Rajas of the Hills around Punjab and the Muslim Mughal ruling class collaborated to kill three of the Gurus; Sri Guru Arjan Dev ji and Sri Guru Tegh Bahdur ji and Sri Guru Gobind Singh ji. The Sikhs were persecuted during the Mughal rule and there were two attempts made at complete genocide of the Sikhs.

The Sikh Gurus explained that what keeps us from realizing Cosmic Unity in ourselves is our Haumain ("I am") consciousness. It is a fragment (Atman) of the Supreme Soul (Param-Atama) or God the Creator embodied within each of us.. There is nothing wrong with having Haumain. It is also a part of the Creation and helps an individual enjoy and experience life as it unfolds for her/him in their embodied spirit. The problem emerges when the individual gets too attached to his/her Haumain experience. One begins to create a sense of duality and begins to feel it is "mine" and it is "yours." One does not stop there. One gets attached to mine and may even become envious of what is yours. One may begin to cultivate power and use it to protect what is mine or to grab what is yours. The spiritual goal is to be steeped in the love of Cosmic Naam consciousness that creates a sense of spiritual unity and reduces Haumain attachment.

After the spiritual guide dies we start a "religion" in his name. Almost all religions end up following the power and Haumain paradigm instead of love and the Cosmic Naam paradigm. The Sikhs are only five hundred years old. The current Sikh religious leaders are almost completely

Haumain oriented. They have become very sectarian and are instituting practices that are quite antithetical to the teachings of the Gurbani. They have killed thousands of people to establish their own state of Khalistan. It is contrary to Gurbani (Guru's verses) that states:

Raj Na Chahoon

Mukt Na Chahoon

Munn Preet Charan Kamla Re

I do not want a kingdom

Nor do I desire salvation

All my mind wants

Is love of your lotus feet

There is a 100% correlation among religions about the essence of spiritual practice. Every spiritual guide has told us that love is the way to please the Divine. No spiritual leader has said that power, exploitation of others and violence pleases the Creator (called by many different names). **Yet, all the religions identify with the aggressor who persecuted these loving souls and became like the power elite of the time.** Anna Freud in her book, Ego and the Mechanisms of Defense, described identification with the aggressor as one of the major psychological defenses. **The followers of the persecuted or murdered spiritual guide identify with the aggressor and become like him, thus betraying their spiritual guide.** These new aggressors used power and violence to subjugate people in the name of religion. They have exploited and treated people brutally in the name of the Creator. **It is time for us to renounce the power paradigm and follow the love paradigm taught by every spiritual guide.** We should not allow the power elite to desecrate the name of the spiritual guides who belong to the whole humanity and not a religion, nation or community.

We need to have intra-faith dialogue with the ruling class in each religion that uses violence in the name of the spiritual guides. The Christians should have intra-faith dialogue with their ruling class and religious elite. Muslims should have intra-faith dialogue with their ruling class and religious power elite. Likewise the other religious communities, such as, Jews, Sikhs, Buddhists, Jains, Zoroastrians etc need to pursue this dialogue with their respective religious and political elite. The purpose of religion is to promote personal spiritual transformation. **We have to realize that by and large all religions have failed their spiritual guides by failing to help their followers in their personal transformation to incorporate the "Loving Spirit" in each of them. In spite of this, there are spiritually oriented individuals in every religion and their numbers are increasing.**

Most interfaith dialogue focuses on the rituals and socio-cultural aspect of religion. These are the manifestation of the historical context of the time of the spiritual guide. These are interesting and we may have a lot of fun with these but this focus keeps us away from the true spiritual message. We have to go beyond the superficial to share spiritual substance and realize our spiritual unity.

In spite of the chaos and cruelty, I feel that the time has come for this paradigm shift. We have the technology and the institutions to deal with fear and the actual threats that we face. Human civilization has developed laws and norms of justice that have become progressively universal. We have infrastructures such as the United Nations and the International Court to govern ourselves according to international law and code of conduct. There is an awakening to promote the paradigm of spiritual love. Pope Paul John II sent a papal message that the days of conversion are gone; now these are the days of collaboration. In almost every city in the United States there are inter-faith groups. Bishop William Swing of Grace Cathedral in San Francisco started the international United Religions Initiative. **We need to lovingly convince our religious and political leaders in every country to become a law-abiding country, promote peace and justice and use non-violent ways to resolve conflicts.** There are skills and knowledge available to resolve conflicts in a peaceful way. We can also have a loving dialogue with our religious institutions to focus on personal transformation to create a loving consciousness in its members and revive the **Loving Spirit.**

6-12-17 Post Script:

1. I notice that there is a repetition of spiritual paradigm in nearly every one of the four articles. I decided to leave this repetition in hoping that it may have some impact. It has been repeated in different contexts and in

different times in my life. I have to remind myself of it every day because the pressure to follow my Haumain pursuits impinge on me daily and makes it hard to be loving.

2. The last half-century of my experience and observations have given me great hope. At present the United Religions Initiative has 858 Cooperation Circles in 101 countries promoting love and peace. Almost every city in the United States has inter-faith organizations. It demonstrates that there is a heightened concern for our mutual survival and motivation to cooperate.

3. In 1958 there was very little political dialogue among my friends. Now there is a great awakening. Every one is talking about our political system all the time and there are millions of activists who show up on our streets and in discussion forums. **My hope is that we can maintain love within ourselves and not be corrupted by power when we get the opportunity to rule ourselves with love and be our "brother's keeper."**

Chapter - V

The Presenting Problem is Never the Problem

Throughout this book I have repeatedly mentioned that developing a deeper understanding of each other requires listening with detachment from any preconceptions about the problem or its solutions, avoiding the use of punitive value judgments and being non-reactive. Deeper understanding includes a compassionate investment to understand not only what a person is saying or the way they are behaving but to understand where the person is coming from. This includes their frame of reference, their vested interest, life experience, the data on which their position or behavior is based and the forces impinging upon them that influence their behavior or political position. Deep understanding takes time, effort, skill and practice. The result is that it brings people together and prevents or even resolves existing conflicts. There are many organizations that provide training in non-violent transaction. There are numerous publications and training programs for non-violent communication including, Active Listening. **Top politicians and decision makers do not encourage the use of such skills to solve most difficult and crucial problems.** Trillions of dollars are spent on arms, strategic military planning and promoting the State Department's agenda. Not a dime is spent to have a Department with expertise in, and put in charge of, peace promotion and conflict resolution. Congressman Dennis Kucinich tried his level best to start a Peace Development agency in U.S. Congress without success. I am providing an outline of my practice and a brief example to introduce my proposed methodology. This is not to explain the consultation process.

My practice is based upon my psychotherapy experience as a psychologist, who has provided community behavioral health consultation to professionals in various human service, academic and business organizations. It is based on the work of Gerald Caplan, M.D., Professor at Harvard School of Public Health. I participated in his training for two semesters in 1963. In 1964 he published his book Principles of Preventive Psychiatry (1964) in which he described his theory and practice of Community Mental Health Consultation. I have been in contact with him during most of my professional career.

By using his theory and practice one can resolve the unconscious theme interference in a problematic human interaction in one or two sessions. I tried to explain his theory by sharing my experience in practicing his method in Community Behavioral Health Consultation and Crisis Intervention (1961). I developed Peer Consultation and Organizational Development Consultation and Supervisory Process and have used them in various aspects of my professional practice. I have also changed the title of this approach from Community Mental Health Consultation to Community Behavioral Health Consultation. I have summarized my work in the forthcoming four volumes of Community Behavioral Health Practice. The following is a very brief example. The purpose is not to describe the process of consultation but to introduce some salient features.

I was invited by the Regional Mental Health Director of a State to deal with a problem of extreme anger toward and frustration with the Director by his consultant staff. His job was to provide consultation to help county mental health programs implement the State's requirements. I spent four hours one morning with the Director and his consultant staff.

I began by asking them to introduce themselves, their job assignments and their expectations of me. In a low-key manner they described a lot of tension in the group. They wanted me to help them to function as a cohesive team but they did not have much hope, feeling that the problems were long standing and deeply rooted.

After this introduction, I asked the Director to draw their organizational chart. Then I requested one of the consultants to give an actual example of consulting with their assigned county administration. During this presentation, through compassionate exploration, it became obvious that the consultant did a lot of work to reach an agreement with the county administration but, without his knowledge, the Director signed a contract with the county administration that was different from what the consultant was working on. In this session, the rest of the time was spent in developing the structures and processes for an effective collaboration between the consultant and the director. By the end of the consultation session, it was decided that the Consultant will bring the contract for the Director's approval and the Director will not be involved directly with the County Administration.

At the end of my consultation, I always ask the consultees to give me a written evaluation of their experience followed by an oral discussion. In this case, some of them felt in the beginning that I was the most insensitive psychologist that they have ever met. It seemed to some that it was dramatically obvious that there was so much anger and tension in the group and that I was totally oblivious to it. But, by the end of the session they felt that something very important was accomplished. They agreed that the core problem creating most of the anger and frustration within the consultants in relationship to the Director was resolved.

I want you to notice that the presenting problem was anger and tension in the group. I could have focused on it by working on anger management. I have learned through my half century of experience that the presenting problem is a symptom. The skill of the consultant lies in the choice of the **focus** of compassionate exploration.

This sounds simple but it is very difficult to do. With whomever I have been invited to consult, they usually have solutions in mind to discuss. Very often they want to focus on interpersonal tensions. In my experience interpersonal tensions are the result of some unresolved issues in the organizational structures and processes. Therefore, in my paper, Beyond Camelot (1975) I described the following conclusion:

> **…. interpersonal tensions, poor morale and low productivity is the result of pressures impinging on an organization and its ability in terms of structures and processes available to the organizations to resolve those pressures.**

This finding has relevance in resolving international problems. For example in the current North Korean problem, Kim Jong-Un is mostly described as a crazy dictator. The proposed solution is to force him by sanctions and threats to give up his nuclear program. The international diplomats feel less hopeful now that Trump has appeared on the scene with his threats. But this policy of threats and sanctions has been going on since the Korean War. Whenever any South Korean leadership has tried to follow a "Sunshine" policy of reconciliation with North Korea the United States threats become more intense.

Do you know that there has not been a peace treaty between the United States and North Korea since the Korean War? It is just a ceasefire. North Koreans want a peace treaty. Why does the United States not want a peace treaty with a nation that is recognized by the United Nations?

How can these parties be brought to the negotiating table? Calling each other names, imposing sanctions and continuing to justify your position cannot resolve any conflict.

The journalists have a most important role - to understand all issues relevant to the presenting problem and focus their questions to "understand" the President's position, instead of following his tweets and having talking heads express their opinions. They should not just be supporting the State Department's policy as "patriots" but represent the people's interest to "understand" in depth the diplomatic position on both sides.

References

Caplan, Gerald (1964), Principles of Preventive Psychiatry – Chapter VIII & IX, Basic Books, New York

Singh, R.K. Janmeja (1961), Community Mental Health Consultation and Crisis Intervention, National Press, Palo Alto

Singh, R.K. Janmeja (1975), Beyond Camelot, Humanliberation-meji. com website.

Chapter - VI

Summary and Conclusions

Causes of Destruction

Perpetual wars, the threat of nuclear holocaust, catastrophic climate change, refugee crises, poverty, the extreme gap between the rich and the poor and paucity of housing, food, health, education and other welfare services are **brought to you** by the multinational corporations, through Madison Avenue, other advertising companies, false think tanks and commercial media. Lobbyists who influence the U.S. Congressional legislation to increase their profits and help elect the Senators and the Congressmen to protect their interests. They also brought you Clinton, Bush, Obama and Donald Trump. **They also brought to you the following:**

1. Cigarettes you were persuaded to smoke by ads showing people laughing and merry making. That cigarettes can kill you was kept secret for years. No body went to jail for such a mass murder.

2. Soft drinks and highly processed fast food that has damaged and even destroyed personal health over the last two generations.

3. Alcohol, illegal and psychotropic drugs. Not only individuals but also states are dependent on their sales for revenue.

4. Chemical fertilizers and nuclear tests that have polluted the environment and cause cancer, immune deficiency diseases and other chronic illnesses.

5. Domestic sales of arms with NRA support. Global sales of arms used by the State Department to influence foreign policy and results in perpetual divisiveness and conflict among peoples.

6. The 2008 economic meltdown with an 11% loss of global wealth. They were bailed out by taxpayer money while millions of persons lost their homes and savings. Their executives, instead of going to jail, were rewarded with hefty bonuses.

7. Stimulation of unnecessary want that promotes unbridled consum-

erism and increases their profits.

8. Manipulation of the government to their benefit, while convincing the public that the government is their enemy.

The people who run these corporations and politicians under their influence are not evil people. They are misguided and unaware of the misery and destruction they cause. Sometimes they use rationalizations to justify their actions. They know not what they do. The author has explained it in terms of every person's struggle within oneself. They are attached to and are motivated by Haumain (I am) or Cain consciousness.

Solutions

1. The problems as presented are seldom the real problem. Focus on finding solutions to the manifest problems does not resolve the real problem. **It is just fighting shadows.** Caught in a preconceived attachment to stereotypical thinking, while promoting democracy, human rights, or prosperity and peace does not lead to a productive outcome. All I can do is to point out what will be required to solve problems in a productive way.

Each problem is very complex. First the parties or persons involved need to collect observable relevant data to develop a common understanding, then work toward solutions. If we have already made up our mind to promote the preconceived agenda of a political party, a country, an economic system or religious beliefs, the result will lead to conflict and probable destruction. The focus needs to be on problem solving rather than the success of a preconceived agenda or faultfinding.

2. All of us are programmed differently. Instead of being attached to our programmed self and trying to convince others that our values, thoughts, religion or country are better than yours, we need to listen to each other with detached and compassionate investment in understanding the other. **Not just what they are saying or the way they are behaving, but where are they coming from is key. What is their experience and frame of reference? What interests do they represent and what facts are they using to formulate their position.** A deeper understanding of each other brings us together. Arguments to persuade drive us apart.

3. All social interactions are symbolic. We need to understand what is the reality behind these symbols.

4. We have to shift from Haumain and Cain consciousness motivation to Naam or a spiritual unity consciousness. Ecologically life on this planet is interdependent. All of us are in it together. We sink or swim together. If we hurt or exploit another for our vested interest we are hurting ourselves.

5. Instead of focusing on the individual and demonizing each other to solve political problems we need to understand the context, system and the processes that produced that individual or that individual's behavior.

6. We need to promote a family environment where **parents have the time and resources to nurture their children to grow up as caring persons.** Equal public education should be provided to everyone to have an egalitarian society where the children learn humanitarian values and not how to just be a commodity in the work force. Providing a different education to different socio-economic level children cannot result in an egalitarian democratic society.

7. We have come a long way. Life is better and the risk of losing it is also greater. **Nations were able to free themselves of foreign occupation. But, now we have realized that our own ruling elite has no interest in the wellbeing of its own people**. We need to create a society where leadership is granted to those not to serve their own, a group or a country's vested interest, but to serve the interest of humanity on our small planet, and make it a heavenly place for all of us.

8. Work toward a true egalitarian democracy. We have learned a lot from our experience on this planet and have come a long way. We know that the usual power manipulation and violence never solves any problem at any level of human interaction. A two or more party system is still a power manipulation system where a majority power group is created to defeat another group. It is divisive. We need to have constituency groupings that are small enough so that the constituents can know their representative. **There is a consensus that we need peace, prosperity and security. People need time and resources to nurture their families. The need a place to live, food, education and health services.** They can elect a person who has a track record of selfless service in their community. That person needs not to represent any party or group's

preconceived agenda. Selection can be for those who can identify underlying problems and have a track record of solving problems in a productive way that helps the community they represent. Take the money and
party politics out of the political system. Like any job application the
candidates should present their qualifications and track record instead
of demonizing each other and exploiting people with false promises
and propaganda. The campaign period needs to be shortened yet allow
constituents sufficient time to assess the qualifications of the candidates
before they vote. There should be a voting day holiday so that every one
can vote.

When I read what I have written so far, my impulse is to believe that
I know what I am talking about. In fact, these writings are intellectual
translation of my lifetime of emotional experience. I am reminded of a
portion of a Punjabi poem that I wrote in January, 1958:

Khiri Basant vich Khizan Di Tasveer Baaki Ai

Duniya De Har hanjhu Vich Teri Tasveer Baaki Ai

......

Surgaan De Sukh Vee Tera Gham Bhula Na Sakde

Jad Tak Eh Dil-e- Dilgir Baaki Ai

In the blooming spring there persists a picture of the Fall

In every tear in the world remains a reflection of your face

......

The heavenly pleasure could never make me forget your suffering

As long as the pain ridden heart still throbs in me

I am just a naked, lost babe, flailing my arms and legs and screaming
with pain in a dark wilderness. Can you comfort me so that I stop crying
and screaming; so that my body will relax and my screaming cease?

Within me I am Donald Trump and the person of color in his audience
who is beaten up and thrown out of his rally.

I am Barack Obama and the grandmother who is blown to smithereens
in front of her grandchildren from his drone strikes.

I am George W. Bush who bombed Democracy into Iraq and Baghdad lit up like a Christmas tree from his incessant bombing. I am an Iraqi who was killed and his country destroyed and a child there who was frightened stiff by the deafening roar of the bombs.

I am Hillary Clinton who bombed Libya, whose country was disintegrated under the guise of being freed from a dictator.

I am Gandhi, Nehru and Jinnah who could not get along with each other and I am a million persons killed and 18 million survivors who lost their ancestral homes, friends and neighbors while seeking freedom from the British.

I could go on and on ad nauseam and my pain will continue and the deafening screams will never cease. Please help me!!!

Biography

Meji was an Adjunct Professor of Psychology for the Doctoral Program in School Psychology at U.C. Berkeley (1991-2007). He was the Founding President of Portia Bell Hume Behavioral Health and Training Center (1993-2001). He was the Dean and Professor of Integrative Psychology at Rosebridge Graduate School of Integrative Psychology (1966-1982). He was the Assistant Director at the Center for Training in Community Psychiatry and Mental health Administration in Berkeley, California (1966-82). For three years he worked for the State Hospitals for mentally ill and for thirty years in Community Mental health Programs. He has provided Organizational Development Consultation to hundreds of organizations across the United Sates.

He received a Lifetime Achievement Award from California State Psychological Association. The United States Congress recognized him for his Fifty Years of Community Service as a Licensed Psychologist. The Surgeon General of the United States Army awarded him a Certificate of Appreciation as a Consultant for developing a Liaison Psychiatry Program and Preventive Services at Letterman Medical Center in Presidio, San Francisco. Oxford Symposium recognized him with an Award for Outstanding Contribution to School-based Family Counseling.

He was the Founding President of Ik Onkar Peace Foundation (2002). It is one of the Cooperation Circles of United Religions Initiative (U.R.I.). At present URI has 850 Cooperation Circles in 101 countries. Meji has been a member of : Rotary Club of Berkeley, California (1983-90); Beyond War Higher Education Group (1987-90); Action Coalition for Global Change, San Francisco (1994-); and Board of Directors, Interfaith Center at Presidio, San Francisco (2001-03).

He was a Founding Member (1964) of the Sikh Center of San Francisco Bay Area, El Sobrante Gurdwara. There he served as Secretary 1973-74 & 1978-79) and Chairperson (1974-75). Meji is a Founding Trustee and has acted as Secretary for The Sikh Foundation of North America, Redwood City, California(1966-74). He served on the Advisory Board (in the Gadar Memorial Task Force) to the Consul General of India, San Francisco (1973-75). He taught Gurbani to Children and Youth at El Sobrante Gurdwara (1991-2004) and served as an International Judge for the Sri Hemkunt Foundation Youth Symposium (1966-2015).

What's Being Said

Building on a life time of painful learning within political and religious turmoil and drawing from his own life long pursuit as an organizational psychologist, Dr. Meji Singh urges us to "wake up and think hard... to shake off the nightmare we have been living in." While nightmare scenarios of being overrun with greed, power, fear and misconceived self interest scare us, we have the choice to wake up and be part of changing the course of destruction. Meji's experiences call us to recognize the problem, and commit to a life pursuit toward more loving consciousness. Nurturing our own loving spirit within a spiritually-centered life is needed to stop the course of destruction. Meji's book points us from despair to love.

Sally Mahé, Co-Director of Global Programs and Organizational Development, United Religions Initiative

Great sages and saints everywhere on this planet struggled to give a vision of the world where inter-illuminating roles of all value-systems and civilizations are possible; a world that recognizes and practices eclecticism. This is what we all know. What is to be done about it, that is a regenerative response. Response pre-figures change. What response to offer in the face of the impossibility of response? How to crusade against the rigidities of human mind? How to shed historical conditioning of solving political problems with violence? How to preserve human capacity to create, to think, to know and to grow?

Meji sahib in this book suggested and recommended multiple ways and means to answer the above questions. He has suggested methods to help human beings to fight against hopelessness and a tragic sense of waste. Multiple maladies of the contemporary human mind demand multiple remedies. One of the remedies that Meji sahib has fervently recommended is to practice the difficult art of loving human beings. Like all arts it needs daily, dedicated and creative practice. According to him, freedom at different levels is a perpetual struggle for all human beings on this planet. He tried to make Freedom an achievable goal for us.

Nabeela Kiani, Professor of English Literature (retired) Government College University, Lahore, Pakistan

My college mate Janmeja Singh is a born intellectual with God gifted skill to analyze. I'm glad he has come out with a book that is based on historical facts and prevalent situations in the World. The World's known ideologies Nationalism, Secularism, Liberal Democracy and Marxism have collapsed. The vacuum created has been filled by religion leading to religious fundamentalism that is leading us to almost a war of civilizations. He introduces Baba Guru Nanak's message of spiritual unity of the universe and to use the spiritual message of all spiritual guides; prophets, Gurus and Avatars for our spiritual transformation so we do not get lost in superficial ritualistic practices. Janmeja offers this as one of the personal efforts that can prevent our sleep walking towards our own destruction.

Tarlochan Singh, Former Member of Parliament (India) and Chairman of the Minorities Commission

Meji examines the world events and personalities to make a point much more global and of everlasting in worth; only a clinical psychologist of his caliber could do it. He scrutinized September Eleven terror attack, the ill-conceived and poorly implemented partition of India, the Hitler phenomena, the intrigues of Vatican and of the Sikh Seat of Authority in India, work force from the money lenders to the labor, the politicians and gullible voters. Meji had his own way of getting into the events from the bottom up, and from the emotional impact, they caused. The readers will undoubtedly find the book as critical reading.

Harbans Lal, Ph.D.; D.Litt (Hons), Professor Emeritus & Chairman, Department of Pharmacology and Neuroscience, U. North Texas. Founding President, Academy of Sri Guru Granth Sahib Studies

Meji's book, Changing the Course of Destruction, tracks the trajectory of mankind's conflict ridden course from the very start of the human existence. The eldest son of Adam and Eve, Cain, got jealous of his brother Abel's closeness to God and killed him. Abel was driven by the love of God and spirituality (which Meji calls "Naam" or "God"), and Cain was driven by ego (which Meji calls "Haumain" or "I am").

The chapters of the book look at the consequences of the "Haumain" driven leaders of the world like Hitler that have inflicted immeasurable sufferings on the human race. The book also highlights many of the "Naam" driven leaders like Moses, Jesus, Mohammed, Buddha, and Guru Nanak who showed the way to spirituality and coexistence.

Meji sees the destruction of our world as imminent unless we change our behavior. We need to try and understand the root causes that drives our adversaries and then resolve our conflicts with the new scientifically proven tools which are now available. Using these proven methodologies and tools the leaders of the world can bring peace and harmony to the conflicted world.

The book is only 145 pages and a delightful read. It has science based solutions, especially for leaders who are genuinely looking for solutions to resolve conflicts and change the course of destruction that we are following now.

Vajid Jafri, Chairman of Mondee, Inc., Chairman and CEO of Onvoya, Inc., and Chairman of the Board of Directors of Portia Bell Hume Behavioral Health and Training Center

'Changing The Course of Destruction' is not just a feeble plea to save the planet - we are used to hearing that; it is not just an isolated voice of the prophet in the wilderness to 'make straight the paths;' it is not just a condemnation of the power and practices of the privileged 'elite' of the world who again and again, age after age, succumb to the lust for power and fame and wealth. It is a sincere call to discover the purpose of human life, as the Creator intended it to be. The book is an outpouring of Dr. Meji's own personal soul-searching; having witnessed depths of human insensitivity and cruelty to each other around the world, he has laid bare the causes, and outlined a course of action to leave the 'Haiman Consciousness' (Ego –centeredness) and follow the 'Naam Conscious-ness' (Other- centeredness) as the most effective and meaningful way to change the course of destruction of our home – Mother Earth.

The book is a must read for everyone who wants to do something per-sonal to make changes in oneself before pontificating for others, a call to develop deeper understanding of the issues of each other before administering solutions; to assess leadership, personal and professional, in terms of the interest in peace, harmony and human values. His reflec-tions of life and spirituality, without religious affiliation offers the world an optimistic perspective, as long as all spiritual practices are aimed at greater awareness of the Creator within oneself and at the same time perceive the Creator in everyone else. For all who know Dr. Meji per-sonally, the reflections and hopes he presents in the book are lived out and practiced personally and proven to bear fruits. May all who read this book, I pray, be blessed by the grace of Kindness, Compassion, and Understanding.

Fr. (Dr.) George Palamattathil SDB
Director, Siloam, India

Dr. Meji Singh's 'Changing the Course of Destruction' delves deep into the realms of human conciousness and explores many interesting questions. Through his writing, Dr. Singh examines variables such as power, control and manipulation and their direct relationship to human pain and suffering. Human concious reflects and manifests social and environmental forces that an individual experiences in day to day interaction. It is obvious that power and control are tools used consistently by elites and so became acceptable norms in the political arena. Throughout human history, these variables were manipulated to subjigate underpriviledged and the disadvantaged.

This book examines these complex variables through objective lenses, taking the reader deep into the core of human problems and offers unique solutions. It also enables the reader to go deeper into human conciousness and learn liberation from the cage of dysfuntional social environements. Problems created by humanity can by solved by humanity. This book gives a sense of direction to the reader to pursue the course of happiness and universal peace.

Khalil Rahmany, Ph.D.
Clinical Psychologist
Author, Where the Bear Met the Lion